annie sloan *Paints*
EVERYTHING

annie sloan
Paints
EVERYTHING

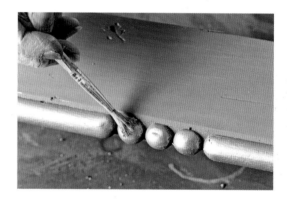

Step-by-step projects for your
entire home, from walls, floors,
and furniture to curtains,
blinds, pillows, and shades

CICO BOOKS
LONDON NEW YORK

I would like to dedicate this book to all of my stockists; I couldn't do this without you. Thanks for all your support and love.

Published in 2016 by CICO Books
An imprint of Ryland Peters & Small Ltd
20–21 Jockey's Fields   341 E 116th St
London WC1R 4BW   New York, NY 10029
www.rylandpeters.com

10 9 8 7 6 5 4 3 2 1

A CIP catalog record for this book is available from the Library of Congress and the British Library.

ISBN: 978-1-78249-356-3

Printed in China

Editor Caroline West
Design concept Geoff Borin
Designer Sarah Rock
Photographer Christopher Drake

Senior editor Carmel Edmonds
Art director Sally Powell
Production manager Gordana Simakovic
Publishing manager Penny Craig
Publisher Cindy Richards

CONTENTS

INTRODUCTION

I don't expect many books have been named after the words printed on a paint-mixing stick, but that's what happened in this case! I was at the planning stage of the book and explaining to my publisher that one of the things I wanted the book to be about was how you can, in fact, paint everything! Across the table were the mixing sticks we had just launched. One thing led to another and the book was named!

Because it is true that, as the book's title suggests, Annie Sloan paints everything! Throughout the preparation of the book, "Paint Everything" has been the rallying cry. But I didn't want it to be about all the weird and wonderful things people paint—skateboards, tubas, and even caravans!—nor just about all the multitude of surfaces that can be painted, such as fabrics, concrete, plastics, melamine, marble, and metal, as well as all the usual surfaces like wood. This is an important point, of course, and one that I certainly took into account: you'll see how I have painted as many different types of wood, both old and new, as I could (namely, oak, mahogany veneer, parquet flooring, scaffolding boards, and pine), along with metals, leather, glass, and fabrics as diverse as lace, burlap (hessian), dust sheets, canvas, and different linens, including my own Annie Sloan Coloured Linens. I even painted rope!

In this book, I wanted to excite you and encourage you to paint everything. I wanted to show how my own range of paint, Chalk Paint®, which I developed in 1990, has retained its classic identity and continued to evolve and develop with new techniques and treatments. It is part of a greater story about interior decorating, involving fabrics, walls, and floor treatments, which can be used to transform your home in a natural and stylish way.

I have gilded and tarnished metal leaf; I have lino-printed on furniture; I have painted, tied, dyed, and dipped fabrics. I have printed, stenciled, and reverse-stenciled on fabrics, walls, and furniture. I have painted in a painterly, freehand way and in a controlled way. I've used colored waxes and crackled paintwork. I've used transferred images and decorated chairs, tables, chests of drawers, lamp bases, and lampshades. And there were still plenty of ideas that didn't make it into the book!

I have been inspired by art and artists, fashion and design, and I've thought inside the box and outside the box, been conventional and unconventional. I have done lots of easy projects and a few projects that will need a little more skill. I decided at an early stage that if a project didn't push my buttons, then it wasn't going in the book. This is also a huge shout-out for the power of color and how colors can be combined. If any thing gets my juices going, then it's how color and texture work together.

I think this is my most personal book yet and it comes very directly from me, with my color palette and style. Please enjoy it, be inspired, and, above all, paint everything!

TOOLS AND MATERIALS

Using the right tools and materials is, of course, absolutely essential if you are to achieve the best results! Everything I've painted in the book uses my Annie Sloan paints and materials.

PAINT

There are many paints on the market, but I have designed the projects in this book with my purpose-made Chalk Paint® in mind (see Useful Addresses on page 158 for stockists). The paint can be applied to most surfaces or used as a dye for fabrics (see www.anniesloan.com for information on unsuitable surfaces). It has a very matte texture and absorbs wax easily, and has been specially created to be used in a huge variety of ways—for example, as a wash, with or without texture, applied thickly, on fabric, or as a dye—which is why it lends itself so well to painting everything.

One of the great bonuses of using this particular paint is that there is no need to prepare furniture first by priming or rubbing down, which means you can start painting easily and quickly while you have the urge. The paint, despite being water-based, even mixes easily with the solvent-based wax too, so you can color the final finish to get the exact color you want. As a general guide, you will need 1-quart (1-liter) cans of paint for large projects and small project pots for painting and decorating smaller areas. For the most part, you only need to apply one coat of Chalk Paint®, but where two coats are necessary, apply the first one with a big brush.

COLOR

Don't be shy to use colors. Color scares most people and suggesting that they use colors can conjure up a circus-like array of hues, so they err on the side of caution and end up with a lot of neutrals, which can be disappointing. Perhaps it would be better to focus on some neutrals and then add some color. For instance, when thinking of what color to paint a piece of furniture for a particular room, you could start with a palette of neutrals with, say, one or two stronger colors for interest and focus. In other words, either paint a piece of furniture in a defined color with neutral walls or vice versa. Remember that colored waxes can change the color too, so take this into consideration when you are applying your chosen paint.

My paints are made so that they can be mixed together, which means you can also create your own colors. To do this, begin by mixing different paints together on paper, in a paint roller tray, or on an Annie Sloan MixMat™. Use your fingers or small brushes to work out the proportions of each color. Once you have determined the ratio of colors, you can go on to make larger quantities, using this as your guide. Start with the greater quantity and then add the second and third colors, testing all the time to see where you are in the mix.

Color is extraordinary as it changes so much according to the context within which it is used—a color that looks great in one room could look like dirty pond water in another because of the light levels (either artificial or natural) and the surroundings. If you are painting a piece of furniture for a particular room, it might be a good idea to make up your paint colors in that room.

If you want clashing colors, then use adjacent primary and secondary colors. These colors can also be mixed together if you wish to make adjustments—for example, add Barcelona Orange to Emperor's Silk to make it more of a tomato-red.

THE COLOR WHEEL

A lot of the color wheels you come across are abstract and technical-looking. For that reason, I have created my own triangular color wheel, using my paint colors. The neutrals are positioned separately. Each neutral is a mix of colors—for instance, Paris Grey is a mix of blue and orange.

To find a color's complementary color, look at its "opposite" color on the other side of the wheel. Facing English Yellow, for example, are Emile and Old Violet. Use a little of either of these to darken English Yellow, or use the two colors together but alter their tonal values by adding Old White. This means that you could have creamy pale yellows alongside lavender/lilac colors, although not in equal amounts. For example, use Old Violet and Old Ochre—which are opposite each other on the wheel—together in a room or on a piece of decoration.

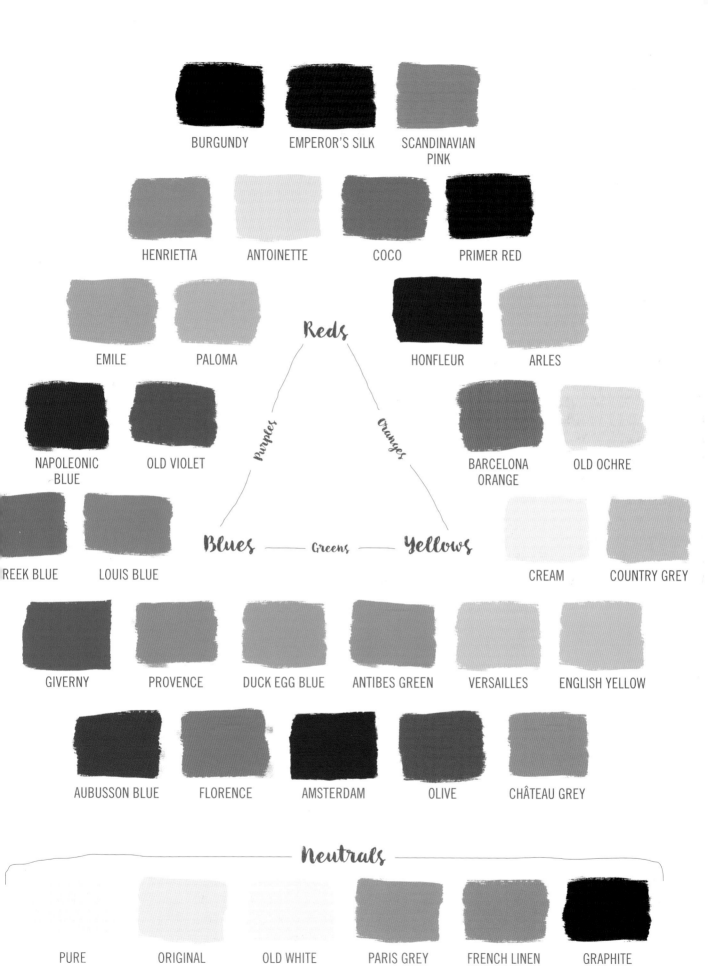

BURGUNDY   EMPEROR'S SILK   SCANDINAVIAN PINK

HENRIETTA   ANTOINETTE   COCO   PRIMER RED

EMILE   PALOMA

Reds

HONFLEUR   ARLES

Purples   *Oranges*

NAPOLEONIC BLUE   OLD VIOLET

BARCELONA ORANGE   OLD OCHRE

REEK BLUE   LOUIS BLUE

Blues — Greens — Yellows

CREAM   COUNTRY GREY

GIVERNY   PROVENCE   DUCK EGG BLUE   ANTIBES GREEN   VERSAILLES   ENGLISH YELLOW

AUBUSSON BLUE   FLORENCE   AMSTERDAM   OLIVE   CHÂTEAU GREY

Neutrals

PURE   ORIGINAL   OLD WHITE   PARIS GREY   FRENCH LINEN   GRAPHITE

BRUSHES

I have created a range of brushes for painting furniture to achieve the wide range of marks, textures, and flat surfaces needed for painting different styles. You can use any brush you wish, but it does need to have certain qualities, because working with bad brushes can be very frustrating. The hairs should be fairly long and flexible, with a little bounce to allow you to be expressive in your work. Don't choose brushes that are too short, since the paint will not flow well, and don't use a brush with hard and inflexible bristles, because the paint will look scratchy. Don't have a floppy brush, because you will have to work too hard to make the paint spread.

Some projects also use artists' brushes. These are soft-haired brushes from artists' suppliers. Cheap craft brushes will only result in frustration, as they are not responsive and the hairs quickly become floppy or fall out. The most expensive artists' brushes are made from sable hair, which are very good, although squirrel hair and high-quality synthetic brushes don't cost as much and work extremely well, offering the right amount of strength and spring.

Throughout this book I have recommended brushes for each project (see Brush Types and Sizes, below), but it's important to pick a size that feels comfortable for you to use and suits the size of the piece of furniture or the wall or floor you're working on.

WAXES, SANDPAPER, VARNISHES, AND CLOTHS

I wax more or less everything I paint to get the right finish for my furniture and walls. It makes my projects strong and practical, and gives them a beautiful, workable finish. I recommend you choose a soft wax that can be applied easily with a brush. I often use a 1in (2.5cm) brush to apply wax, but you can use a large brush to get it done quickly if that feels more comfortable. After adding a layer of clear wax to a piece, you can then start applying dark wax or coloring the clear wax with some of my paint to alter the finish. (For details on different waxes, see Types of Wax, opposite.)

For the distressed look, or for achieving a very fine finish, you need to be able to sand the waxed surface to reveal the wood or another coat of paint—so have a range of fine-, medium-, and coarse-grade sandpapers at hand for this purpose. I produce an Annie Sloan range of Sanding Pads in all three grades. I find that using just the fine and medium grades is usually enough, but sometimes move on to the coarser paper if I really want to distress the furniture.

The only time I use varnish is on floors, when I am doing découpage, and for transfer work. I prefer to apply wax to my work at the end because it has such a soft finish, can be colored and changed as you work, and stops the work chipping.

Make sure you also have a good supply of cloths: use old rags for general use and clean, dry, lint-free cloths for

BRUSH TYPES AND SIZES

Where possible, I suggest you use my range of brushes. In addition to the Annie Sloan brushes listed below, I also use a selection of artists' detail brushes. For the projects in this book, I have used the following equivalents:

OVAL BRISTLE BRUSHES
Annie Sloan Pure Bristle Brushes in Small, Medium, and Large

FLAT BRUSHES
Annie Sloan Flat Brushes (made of synthetic fibers) in Small and Large

WAX BRUSHES
Annie Sloan Wax Brushes (made of pure bristle) in Small and Large

STENCIL BRUSH
Annie Sloan Stencil Brush (made of pure bristle)

TYPES OF WAX

My Annie Sloan range also includes a selection of waxes, which are used in some of the projects, as follows:

CLEAR WAX
Annie Sloan Clear Soft Wax

DARK WAX
Annie Sloan Dark Soft Wax

BLACK WAX
Annie Sloan Black Chalk Paint® Wax

WHITE WAX
Annie Sloan White Chalk Paint® Wax

removing excess wax, polishing, wiping brushes, applying and wiping off paint, and general cleaning.

ADDITIONAL ITEMS

These items are not essential, but I use them regularly and they will prove helpful for many of the projects in the book:
• Table protector
• Paint roller tray
• Annie Sloan MixMat™
• Mixing stick
• Pencil
• Sketchpad
• Scissors
• String
• Yardstick (meter ruler)
• Tape measure
• Masking tape
• Sponge rollers (the Annie Sloan range includes small and large)
• Latex (rubber) gloves (entirely optional, as these are not something I use)

The following items are used less regularly, but are needed for specific projects:
• Lino cutter
• Hot glue gun
• Annie Sloan Coloured Linen (for soft-furnishing projects)
• Batting (wadding)
• Iron and ironing board
• Stencils (see the Annie Sloan stencil range)
• Stencil brush
• Annie Sloan Découpage Glue and Varnish
• Water-based gold size, such as Annie Sloan Gold Size
• Lacquer, such as Annie Sloan Lacquer
• Annie Sloan Craqueleur
• Large sponge (for cleaning large surfaces)
• Newspapers (for the frottage technique)
• Old pail (bucket) or bath tub (for dyeing projects)

CHAPTER 1

FURNITURE AND LIGHTING

Discover imaginative pieces of furniture with each one painted using a different technique, including stenciling, painterly paint, gilding, and distressed paint. Included are dining tables, as well as a coffee table and console table, chairs, a French-style sofa, chests of drawers, a wooden lamp, and a brass chandelier. Styles range from classic to contemporary, with graphic, warehouse-rustic, and folk influences, among others.

LINO-PRINT CHAIR

I'm very fond of this type of chair because it lends itself to so many techniques. This is the story of how the painting of a piece of furniture can evolve—I often know exactly what I want to do; at other times, the piece develops more slowly.

I needed a blank canvas to start with, as the dark wood was distracting, so I painted the chair in Paris Grey, a classic, mid-tone color that is neither dark nor light. Painting with a neutral color such as this is a good idea as it provides a perfect base for bright or pale colors. The chair now looked acceptable, but needed a little more to make it interesting. I tried frottage (a word I use to describe the technique of rubbing crumpled-up newspaper over a thin wash of paint—see page 152) in Greek Blue and the effect was great.

I still wasn't convinced, though, so I left the chair alone for a while. I went on a lino-printing workshop and returned with a design of a cup and saucer. Lino printing is a method used by many artists, including Picasso and Matisse, and was very popular in the 1950s. It's recently returned to favor, as it has a retro look but, best of all, the hard, old lino has been replaced by a softer material that's very easy to use.

I found my teacup design used upside down worked very well, as it looked quite abstract, and that I could wrap the lino around the chair legs and back. I used the oval part of the design to create a symmetrical focus, while the textured pattern of the rest of the design combined well with the frottage to give a random but even effect.

YOU WILL NEED

- Chalk Paint® in Napoleonic Blue, Paris Grey, and Greek Blue
- Pencil
- Piece of soft-sided lino
- Lino cutter
- Small flat brush
- Sketchbook
- Medium oval bristle brush
- Paint roller tray
- Newspaper
- Small wax brush
- Clear wax
- Clean, dry, lint-free cloths

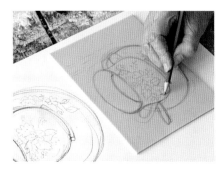

1 Make a drawing of whatever you want to feature on the piece of furniture, whether this is abstract or naturalistic, copied or taken from a book. Trace the drawing onto the lino with a pencil (you can also draw the design freehand if you wish).

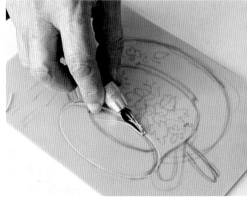

2 Take the lino cutter and dig gently and smoothly into the lino. I cut some of the lines twice (i.e. a double line) to strengthen and emphasize the design. Remember that you can always go over the cutting again once you've done a test print.

3 Once you are happy with your design, use the small flat brush to paint a thin, but undiluted, coat of Napoleonic Blue onto your lino print.

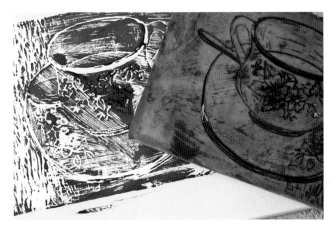

4 Do a test print in your sketchbook to check that you are happy with the effect. Make sure you press down gently and evenly. Some people like to use a roller to make sure the pressure is applied evenly.

5 Use the oval bristle brush to paint the chair in Paris Grey—I painted every which way to create texture. Paris Grey started out as a mid-tone, but ended as the lightest tone, against the bright Greek Blue and the deep Napoleonic Blue.

6 Once the coat of Paris Grey is completely dry, add a small amount of water to some Greek Blue in the paint roller tray to create a thin paint. It should be quite drippy.

7 Using the oval bristle brush, apply a thin layer of the diluted Greek Blue over the Paris Grey. (You should still be able to see the gray underneath.)

8 Scrunch and crinkle up some newspaper and lay it flat on the painted surface. There should still be some crinkles left in the newspaper.

9 Push the newspaper down and then quickly peel it off. Repeat quickly over the rest of the chair, remembering to work into the joins.

10 Take the piece of lino, paint it with Napoleonic Blue (or a color of your choice), and position it on the chair. I placed the print upside down in some areas to create a design that is a little more abstract and interesting.

11 Keep printing until you are happy with the overall look. I added stripes down the side of my lino design to create some variation in the image. The lino can be wrapped around the chair splats to create different patterns.

12 Once the paint has dried, use the wax brush to apply clear wax to the chair. Remove excess wax with a clean cloth.

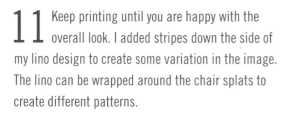

TEXTURED PAINT RADIOGRAM

This is a real bit of upcycling using a piece of furniture that would have been the pride and joy of many a living room in the 1950s, but has now been replaced by a pocket-sized gadget. It's a radiogram in the guise of a very baroque and grand piece of furniture, and would originally have held 78 RPM records, a record player (then called a gramophone), and a radio. The tabletop lid opened up to reveal all the musical paraphernalia, although this had all been removed by the time I got hold of the radiogram. I love the overall shape and the extravagant ball-and-claw feet in particular.

I replaced the grille in the front from which the sound originally emanated with a piece of wood and then painted the walnut veneer. The radiogram is now used as a side table, with just two small cupboards in the front.

YOU WILL NEED

- Chalk Paint® in Old White
- Medium oval bristle brush
- Clear wax
- 2 small wax brushes
- Clean, dry, lint-free cloths
- Dark wax

1 Since this piece of furniture is large, I painted it in sections in Old White with the oval bristle brush, applying the paint thickly to create texture.

2 Leave for a short while—this time will vary according to how thick the paint is, how thickly you applied it, and the ambient temperature. While the paint is still wet, but beginning to dry, work the brush back into the paint to create even more texture. Apply just a little pressure as your brush glides over the paint, pulling the top layer unevenly over the drying paint beneath to create troughs and pits. Also add a little more paint to the brush, so that fresher, wetter paint is pulled over the drying paint below. Allow to dry naturally.

TIP

The Old White paint is quite thick and you may get a little impatient after painting such a large piece of furniture, so use a hairdryer to speed up the drying process. This may create some cracks in the paint, but this makes for a little more interest in the texture.

3 Once the paint is dry, apply clear wax using one of the wax brushes, working the wax in well with the points of the brush to ensure it reaches into all the crevices and pits. Use a cloth to remove any excess. This wax seals the paint.

4 While the clear wax is still wet, apply the dark wax with the other wax brush. It's important to apply the dark wax in sections.

5 The dark wax needs to begin drying out for a minute or so, then as much of the dark wax as possible needs to be wiped off, leaving it in the recesses. This will reveal all the texture in the paintwork. The Old White paint will now look quite brown, so quickly move on to the next step.

6 Use a fresh cloth to apply clear wax to clean off the dark wax. Keep applying the clear wax until the surface is clean and the dark wax only remains in the recesses. Don't allow the dark wax to dry out, because it can be difficult to remove if this happens.

7 Apply a fresh coat of clear wax using the wax brush, and then make a translucent mix of water and Old White and brush this over the still-wet clear wax with the oval bristle brush.

8 Take another cloth and gently wipe this over the piece of furniture, so that the paint and wax mix together to create a misty white glaze—this will help to soften and give a clean look to the furniture.

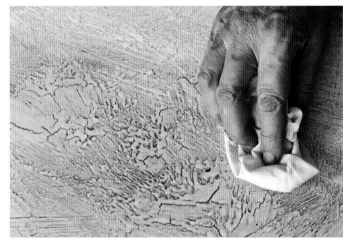

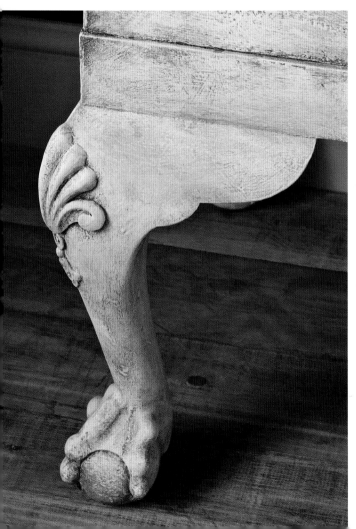

REVERSE STENCIL FOLK TABLE

I wanted a rustic design for this country-cottage table. I tried painting the table with Country Grey, but the result did nothing for me. However, as I began washing off the paint with a sponge and water, I noticed that the table looked good and so I left it mainly painted, but with some wood showing through in places.

I wanted to add a large design to the table, based on the idea of cut-out paper because, as a child, I had folded paper and snipped out shapes, delighting in the wonderful, doily-shaped snowflakes that were revealed as I unfolded the paper. These paper designs remind me of Eastern European paper cutouts and the inventiveness of Polish cut paperwork in particular. My interpretation of this paperwork is inspired by the simple, flattened silhouette designs that the technique requires.

I used dancing "girls" as the main design, opting for a figure at each end of the table, and added other shapes around the edge. The result is a unique table that I definitely want to keep.

YOU WILL NEED

- Chalk Paint® in Country Grey, Antibes Green, Aubusson Blue, Provence, and Greek Blue
- Large sponge
- Tabloid-size/A3 heavy card stock/cartridge paper (100 lb/220 gsm)
- Pencil
- Strong scissors
- Small flat brush
- Large stencil roller
- Small stencil roller
- Large artists' brush
- Coarse-grade sandpaper
- Clear wax
- Small wax brush
- Clean, dry, lint-free cloths

1 Paint the table in Country Grey. Once the paint is dry, take a damp/wet sponge and rub away some of the paint to expose the surface beneath.

2 Take a piece of card stock (cartridge paper) and fold it in half, then draw half the design on the paper, using the photos (on the previous page and above) as a guide. Using the scissors, cut out the design while it is still folded in half.

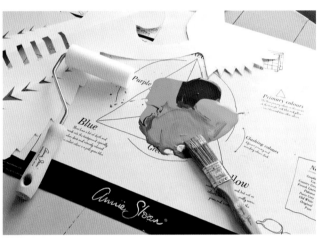

3 Fold the paper again along the front and sides of the dress shape, and cut out more shapes. Here, I cut out a series of rectangles and some arrow shapes. I also cut out a right-angled triangle at the bottom of the paper to create the feet of the figures.

4 Use the flat brush to mix Antibes Green and Aubusson Blue, softened with some Provence, but not too perfectly so that the color will be a little varied when you roll it out.

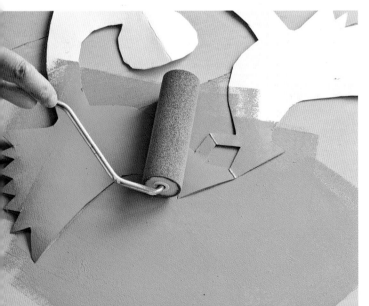

5 Position the paper figure at the top of the table so that the feet are in the center. The idea is to block out the Country Grey with the paper figure. Load the green paint mix onto the large roller and cover the card design so that there is a small border all around the edge. Repeat with the paper figure at the other end of the table. Use the roller to paint the rest of the table, leaving a circular border of Country Grey around the edge.

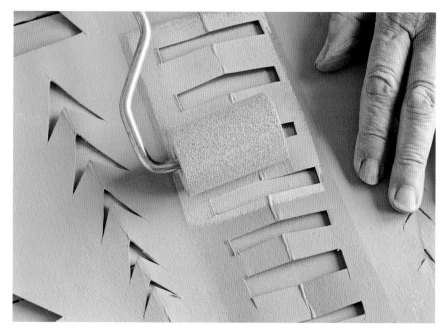

6 To bring out the pattern of the dresses, load the small roller with Greek Blue and carefully place the cut-out rectangular stencils over the matching shapes on the table top, then cover in Greek Blue. I also used the Greek Blue to fill in the diamond shape at the top of each figure. Use the small roller loaded with Country Grey on the rectangular and arrow-shaped stencils to add patterns by the sides of the two dancing figures.

7 Use the lid from the can of wax as a circular template, tracing around it with the artists' brush to paint the rim of the table with Provence randomly mixed with Antibes Green and Aubusson Blue. This helps to create depth. Paint a mix of Provence and Antibes Green with a little Aubusson Blue around the molded edge of the table and then distress the edge a little with the sandpaper. Finish by applying clear wax to the table with the wax brush. Use a cloth to remove excess wax and also to polish the table, if you wish.

SMOOTH AND TEXTURED CABINET

I sometimes call this "The Scottish Cabinet" because I was inspired to paint it after visiting an exhibition, in Edinburgh, on two Scottish artists, Robert McBryde and Robert Colquhoun, who painted in the 1940s and '50s. What their work revealed was the way in which the paint was used both with and without texture, and I realized that I could do something similar with my paint. The whole piece has been done with a variety of finishes. Some areas are sanded very smoothly and some are textured with dark wax and washes too. I also made use of the way the pencil lines smudge and made them thicker in places. I took my lead from the two Roberts and did an abstract scene of buildings, but, if you don't feel up to this, then a design of stripes or checks could be used instead, as I have done on the drawer front. My scene was also partly inspired by the triangular, art-deco-shaped handles, which I echoed in my drawing.

YOU WILL NEED

- Chalk Paint® in Old White and Napoleonic Blue

- Small project pots of Chalk Paint® in: Arles, Antibes Green, Barcelona Orange, Paris Grey, Coco, Versailles, Graphite, Scandinavian Pink, and Château Grey

- Small or medium oval bristle brush

- Soft pencil (such as 3B or 4B)

- Mixing stick or ruler

- Variety of artists' brushes

- Small flat brush

- Small wax brush

- Clear wax

- Clean, dry, lint-free cloths

- Dark wax

- Annie Sloan MixMat™

- Fine- or medium-grade sandpaper

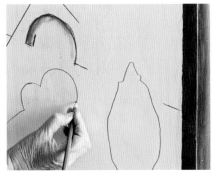 

1 Paint the door in Old White, adding a little texture by using the oval bristle brush to create brush marks. When the paint is dry, draw the design clearly on the cabinet with the pencil—draw some of the lines freehand and use a mixing stick or ruler to draw the straight lines. You can easily paint out any mistakes that you make when drawing.

2 Plan ahead before you start creating the smooth and textured areas, as you may find it easier to finish each of the different textures in one go, rather than jumping from one technique to another. To create the textured areas, use a square-ended, bristle artists' brush to dab on Old White with a stippling motion to give the paint texture. Here, I'm working on the sky area, but I also created the effect on other parts of the design such as the drawers.

3 To create smooth areas, mix a color with some water and apply it to those areas you want to be without texture. Use the flat brush to apply the paint. I prefer some areas to be a little darker and others a little lighter, as this helps add depth. Work over the rest of the design so that everything is either with or without texture.

4 Use the wax brush to apply clear wax all over one of the textured areas.

5 To color the textured area, use an artists' brush to apply a diluted mix of color while the clear wax is still wet. Simply dilute the paint with water until you are happy with the color.

6 Wipe off the diluted paint with a cloth, allowing it to go into the texture of the paintwork. If the paint gets too dark or heavy, then wipe it off with a gentle application of clear wax.

7 Take a small brush and add a flat coat of Château Grey (the brush I used had a little Primer Red in it). I always take advantage of these little mishaps because they add character to a piece.

8 To combine dark wax and a colored wash (and achieve a deep and colored finish), apply clear wax with the wax brush in the required areas.

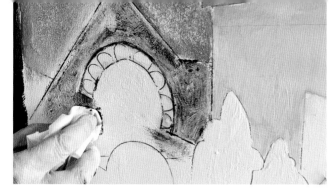

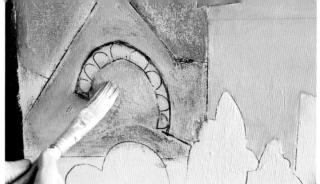

9 Use a cloth to rub dark wax onto the surface, removing any excess as you go along. You can use clear wax to gently erase any undesired dark wax at the end.

10 On the MixMat™, make a mix of Old White, Château Grey, and Antibes Green to cover the areas of dark wax, gently washing it over with a brush and wiping it off in places to add variation. (Remember that Antibes Green is a very strong color—you can add Château Grey to darken it and Old White to soften it.)

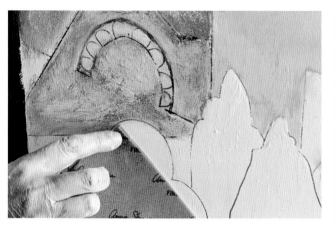

11 To make an area very smooth and flat, simply rub it with the sandpaper.

12 Apply a wash of paint in a color of your choice over this very smoothly sanded area.

TILE-EFFECT STENCIL TABLE

I am interested in the idea of fusing different styles together and this is what I have done here; as is the case in most homes, there is always a certain amount of compromise. Here the three design elements—the table, the chairs, and the stencil pattern—are all quite different, but they result in a contemporary look when combined. The table is a standard one from the 1970s, which was initially inspired by a now very collectible Danish designer. However, the central slat is much higher in this table than in the original design.

The chairs are modern interpretations of Windsor-style farmhouse chairs, while my Tallulah stencil was inspired by Eastern European folk-art, especially the embroidery pieces in which quite a lot of color would be used. So, three very different styles—how to make them work! I decided to put all the color into the chairs and to keep the table and stencil light and subtle. In fact, in certain lights the stencil is hardly visible. To give the stenciling a gentle subtlety, I varied the gray as I stenciled, adding a little more Paris Grey in places.

YOU WILL NEED

- Chalk Paint® in Pure and Paris Grey
- Annie Sloan MixMat™
- Large flat brush
- 1 yardstick (meter ruler) and string, to find the center of the table
- Poster tack
- Annie Sloan Tallulah stencil
- Pencil
- Small stencil roller
- Rag cloth, for removing paint
- Clear wax
- Small wax brush
- Clean, dry, lint-free cloths

1 Paint the table very smoothly with Pure paint. The look I wanted to achieve with the stenciling was an almost white on white. Working with the paints on the MixMat™, it took many tries to get the color exactly right. Starting with Pure, add a little Paris Grey to change the color very slightly and then use the flat brush to test out the color on paper first to ensure the tones are right.

Being an oval table, I needed to find the center before I could start work. I did this by using a yardstick (meter ruler) and string stretched across the table's longest length. Use some poster tack to keep the taut string in place. When you start stenciling, place the tile design in the exact center of the table and then work outward.

2 Find the center of the table (see Tip, right). Line up the stencil, ensuring it's in the exact center of the table; you can use a pencil to mark the table gently, but don't leave an obvious mark.

3 Load the paint onto the roller and hold the stencil in position. Go over the stencil two to three times, making sure you cover the stencil completely.

4 Use the rag cloth to wipe the paint off the stencil, so that you can line up the next stencil print. Use the ruler to align and position the stencil correctly again.

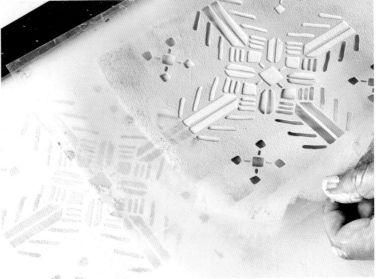

5 To create the illusion of light, shadow, and depth, add a tiny bit more Paris Grey to the paint mix as you stencil. Once you have applied the stenciling to the whole table and it is completely dry, apply clear wax with the wax brush. Remove excess wax with a clean cloth.

WHITE WAX BUREAU

Oak is a very distinctive wood that is characterized by a deep grain. It also has interesting irregular markings, depending on how it is cut. I particularly love oak when it's very old, unvarnished, and natural because it is a lovely, soft, light gray in color. Sadly, in my opinion, pieces from the 1940s are often spoilt by being stained dark and coated in varnishes. This makes the wood look heavy and obliterates the beautiful grain. Similarly, many modern pieces are stained so that they look yellowish and shiny.

The idea with this project is to bring out the natural grain of the oak by putting white wax in the grain, but leaving the smooth wood free of wax. The finished result is a light-looking piece enhanced by a fairly obvious grain.

This particular bureau is from the 1940s or so, and had been lightly varnished with a dark color. The grain was still textural, but the wood was darker than I would have liked. I could have removed the varnish—a rather long and tedious job—but this would have made the whole piece lighter. So, instead, I opted for the easier method of applying white wax to lighten the varnish and bring out the grain of the wood. If I had taken the varnish off, the finished effect would have been a lot lighter and the grain probably more pronounced.

The trick is to allow the wax to harden for long enough that it hardens a little in the grain, but not for so long that the wax does not come off where you want it to.

YOU WILL NEED

- White wax
- Small wax brush
- Clean, dry, lint-free cloths
- Clear wax
- Annie Sloan Valeska stencil and a project pot of Graphite paint, to decorate the edge of the bureau's desk (optional)

1 Take the wax brush and apply a generous amount of white wax, working it both across and in and up and down the wood. Make sure you get the wax into the indents of the grain. Some of the indents may be quite deep and so it may take a few brushstrokes to fill them. Leave to set for 1–3 minutes, so that the wax can harden a little.

2 Use a clean cloth to wipe off the excess white wax lying on top of the wood, leaving the wax in the indents. If you find you're removing too much wax and there is nothing in the grain, simply re-apply the white wax and leave to harden again. Use a clean cloth to ensure the wax is rubbed in well. You can use a tiny bit of clear wax to remove any unwanted white wax that has hardened.

3 Apply more white wax with the brush to the handles and any metal work—there is no need to remove these first. Wipe off the wax with a cloth before the wax dries.

RIGHT I used my Valeska stencil to paint two lines in Graphite to create a decorative border of crosses.

MAKING AN ARC

I came to do this piece after painting a huge circle on a wall of stacked furniture for some exhibitions. On taking the wall apart, I noticed how good each piece looked painted with an arc. I loved the simplicity of the effect and how the focus became the two colors. So, I started thinking about how I could create a large arc on a single piece of furniture. To make the arc large, you need a pivot point outside the chest of drawers. I achieved this by lifting the chest of drawers onto a second chest. I used a project pot tied with a loop of string as my pivot, tied a pencil to the other end of the string, and drew a line. For this mid-century piece, I chose two colors that were popular in the mid-1960s. Putting a pink and an orange together was daring back then. Other combinations from the 1950s and '60s would be English Yellow and Louis Blue, or Scandinavian Pink and Giverny.

YOU WILL NEED

- Chalk Paint® in Antoinette and Barcelona Orange
- String
- Small project pot or round object, to act as a pivot
- Pencil
- Small flat brush
- Large flat brush
- Clear wax
- Large wax brush
- Clean, dry, lint-free cloths

1 Before you start making the arc, paint the chest of drawers all over with Antoinette and allow to dry. Raise your chest of drawers up high, so that you can make the center of your "circle" outside the piece you are painting. Make a large loop in a length of string and attach one end to the project pot and the other end to the pencil. Find your pivot point and then use the string to guide the line of the arc.

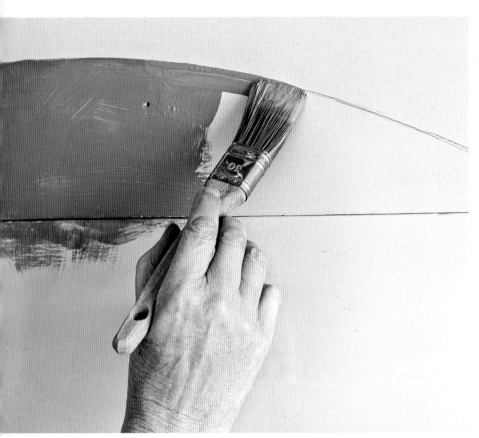

2 Paint the edge of the arc very carefully in Barcelona Orange, using the small flat brush, to get a really smooth, clean, consistent edge.

TIP

If your piece of furniture has handles, then make sure you remove these before you start painting.

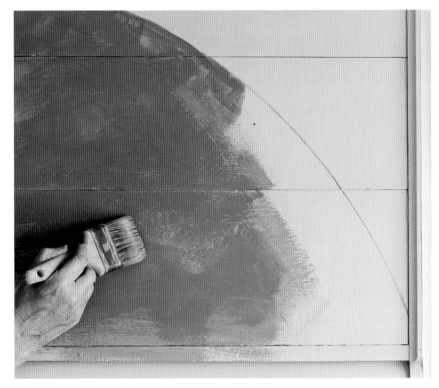

3 Paint the rest of the circle in Barcelona Orange using the large flat brush. Once the arc of paint is thoroughly dry, apply some clear wax with the wax brush. Remove excess wax with a clean cloth.

BLACK-WAXED JAPANESE-STYLE TABLE

When I found this reproduction table in a secondhand store, I was immediately drawn to its shape. I've loved pieces of Japanese art for years and, in fact, have some Japanese prints from a collection of woodblocks I inherited from my father. This table reminded me of the Shinto shrines I saw on a visit to Japan. These temples begin with a doorway that's similar in shape to this table. The doorway roof/tabletop both have upturned ends and a cross bar, while the pillars/table legs are gently splayed. The entrance to a shrine is often colored, usually with vermilion—a bright color that is anywhere between orange, red, and watermelon pink—and also with black in parts. The surface is often shiny and smooth, but I decided to give this table a more textured finish reminiscent of a traditional, Japanese lacquered piece of furniture. Old lacquer has a rich patina and texture, which I knew I could re-create by texturing the Barcelona Orange and using both clear wax and black wax in the texture. The difference in color is achieved by using black wax without any clear wax underneath. For the main part of the table, I used clear wax and then black wax, to give a lighter color, while for the sides and legs of the table I only used black wax to create a much deeper color.

YOU WILL NEED

- Chalk Paint® in Barcelona Orange
- Large oval bristle brush
- Clear wax
- Large wax brush
- Black wax
- Small wax brush
- Clean, dry, lint-free cloths

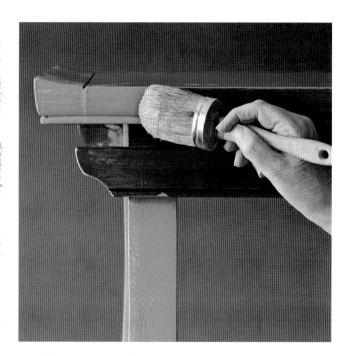

1 Paint the whole table in Barcelona Orange using the oval bristle brush, painting every which way to create texture, but not to an excessive degree.

2 Paint a second coat by holding the brush upright and making sure that the paint is fairly thick. Press hard at first and then feather out by lightening the pressure on the brush and going every which way with long strokes. This will achieve a lightly textured effect. Allow the table to dry.

3 Apply clear wax with the large wax brush to the tabletop, front and back edges, and cross bar, but not to the top side edges or legs where black is wanted.

4 Use the small wax brush to apply black wax to the whole table. Start with the areas that will eventually be black, applying the black wax directly to the painted areas where no clear wax has been applied. This will ensure that these areas will be dark.

5 While the clear wax is still "wet," apply the black wax to the rest of the table. Do this in workable areas of approximately your arm's stretch. Go on to the next step very quickly.

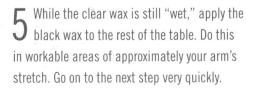

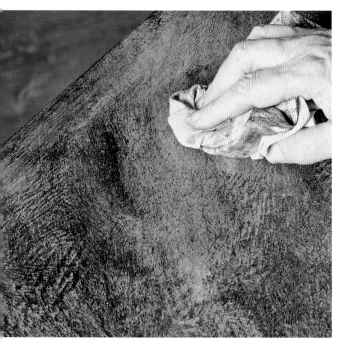

6 While it's still wet, wipe off the excess black wax with a clean cloth from the areas that won't be dark. This should take a lot of wax off, while allowing it to stay in the recesses. Move on to the next step as soon as you can.

7 Use a cloth to apply clear wax and wipe it off these areas. This wax acts like an eraser, leaving your surface clear with some black wax in the grooves of the paintwork and some areas very clean and orange-colored.

8 Finally, after leaving the black-waxed areas (i.e. the top side edges and legs) for approximately 5 minutes, or until the wax has begun to dry out a little (this will depend on the ambient temperature), wipe the black wax to rub it into the surface of the wood, removing any excess and taking it down to the orange paint in places.

9 Leave the table overnight and polish it the next day with a clean, dry cloth until it shines. By this time the solvents in the black wax will have evaporated and the wood will be easy to polish. Where the black wax has been applied generously, it may take longer to harden.

OMBRÉ COFFEE TABLE

Ombré means "shaded" in French, and the gradual blending of colors on pieces of furniture seems to be a crossover idea from the world of fashion, where hair or clothes are dipped into a dye to change their color. Furniture painted in this way is sometimes also called *ombré* or dipped, and refers to pieces where the color changes gradually from one to the other. It's usually the legs of the piece that are treated in this way, since they lend themselves easily to the technique.

The colors should merge seamlessly, so choose colors that work well together when they are mixed. I chose two colors near each other on the color wheel to be sure they would look good when blended. Many people opt for a color with white, so that the color made in between is a pastel. Some color combinations are less successful, however. Choosing, say, blue and yellow means you'd have a band of green in between, which would be distracting.

This little table is fairly featureless, but I thought I would draw attention to the legs, which are sweetly pointy. Although the technique looks easy, it was quite difficult to achieve on this particular table because the legs are angled. Rounded legs would have been easier to paint.

YOU WILL NEED

- Chalk Paint® in Amsterdam Green, Provence, and Old White
- 2 medium oval bristle brushes
- Clear wax
- Large wax brush
- Clean, dry, lint-free cloths

1 Paint the lower half of the table legs with Amsterdam Green using one of the oval bristle brushes.

2 Paint the other half of the legs with Provence using the other brush.

3 Blend the two colors where they meet in the middle of the table legs to create a mid-tone. To blend, stroke very gently and, if anything dries, alternate the brushes with the two colors.

4 Paint the top of the table in Provence and wait until the paint is almost dry before you blend. I added some Old White to the top of the table to lighten it and create a cloudy effect. Once the paint is dry, apply clear wax to the table with the wax brush. Remove excess wax with a clean cloth.

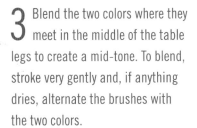

TRANSFER IMAGE CHAIR

I love the way this chair has turned out, particularly as it presented a large slab of brown, uninteresting wood with a leatherette seat that had seen better days. In fact, the large expanse of wood that forms the back of the chair provided a space to make a big design statement. The chair was transformed and now I want more like this! Painting the chair in Greek Blue and adding one large image to the back has brought out its design potential.

My son Felix created an abstract design for me using a computer design program. The image was large enough to cover the chair panel, but had to be printed in two halves on smaller sheets, which were then joined together to cover the whole panel. I wanted the image to be slightly larger than the panel, so that it would not require any cutting down to size. If you created a smaller image, then you would need to cut out the white border around it.

YOU WILL NEED

- Chalk Paint® in Old White and Greek Blue
- Small flat brush
- Sandpaper (optional)
- Pencil, for marking the center line
- Image of your choice to transfer, printed on ordinary computer printer paper
- Scissors (optional)
- Annie Sloan Découpage Glue and Varnish
- Clean, dry, lint-free cloths
- Clear wax
- Small wax brush
- Large flat brush

1 Use the small flat brush to paint the back of the chair in Old White, making sure your paintwork is smooth with no brush marks. Sand lightly if necessary. Mark the center of the chair so you will know where to put each of the sheets of the design.

2 Place the first of the two transfer images the right way up (i.e. with the image uppermost) and cover it with découpage glue. Take care not to get any of the glue on the reverse.

3 Position the image, with the picture side facing down on the chair panel, making sure the edge of the sheet is positioned along the center line. Repeat Step 2 with the other transfer image sheet to cover the rest of the panel. Let dry overnight.

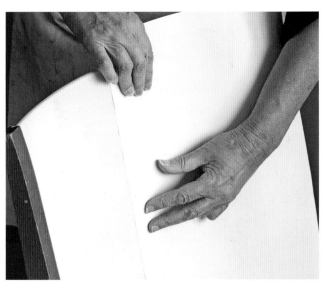

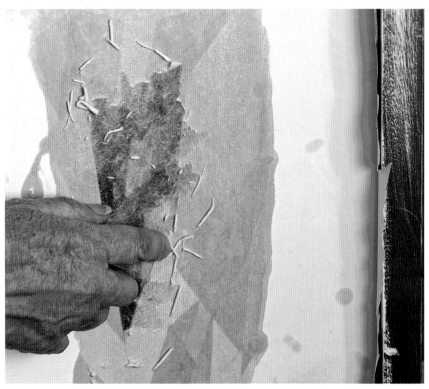

4 To remove the transfers, apply water all over the paper with your fingers and remove the top layer by pushing your index finger forward, so gently easing off the paper. Take care not to work one area too much or you will break the image and go through to the paintwork underneath. Keep wetting your hands as you go along. Use a cloth to help you remove the paper. Let dry. You will find that some areas are still very white with paper, so re-dampen and remove these.

5 The image will still not be very clear, but the application of clear wax will reveal the design. Paint the rest of the chair first in a color of your choice—I used Greek Blue—and then apply clear wax with the wax brush over the image and the chair. Remove excess wax with a clean cloth.

WET PAINT DRAWING

This technique was developed after some experimentation by drawing through paper on a freshly painted piece of furniture. In fact, I thought the effect would be different to the result I actually got, but I like the look I achieved. As I drew on the paper, the paint was pushed to the side and made a wonderful line. Finding the right paper is essential for this project, because it mustn't be too absorbent. I experimented with several types of paper before I found the right type.

For the design you need something that is quite decorative all over, and also very linear—that is, it should be made up of clear lines. This piece was inspired by the December 2014 issue of *World of Interiors* magazine, which featured the mud hut villages of Hazaribagh, in North India. In the spring and fall (autumn), the huts are emblazoned with beautifully bold murals and I found these very inspiring. The lines are clear and strong, and very decorative. The result of drawing on wet paint through the paper is a worn, delicate image with a printed or woodcut quality, where more of the paint is removed in some places than others. The trick is to work quickly and be free with your drawing.

YOU WILL NEED

- Chalk Paint® in Amsterdam Green and Duck Egg Blue
- Small oval bristle brush
- Piece of paper
- 4B pencil
- Small flat brush
- Clear wax
- Small wax brush
- Clean, dry, lint-free cloths

1 Use the oval bristle brush to paint one coat of Amsterdam Green on the surface of your piece of furniture. I'm using a textured brush here, but it doesn't have to be overly textured.

2 While the paint is drying, sketch out your design on the piece of paper. I used a 4B pencil because it is dark and soft, and makes a wide mark. Make sure the paint you are using isn't too absorbent. Only work in one area at a time; otherwise, the paper will stick to the paint if it is left on too long or if it's too absorbent.

3 Use the flat brush to paint your first section with a layer of Duck Egg Blue and then place the drawing on top of it.

4 Go over your hand-drawn design with the pencil, pressing quite hard and then lifting off the paper as soon as you can.

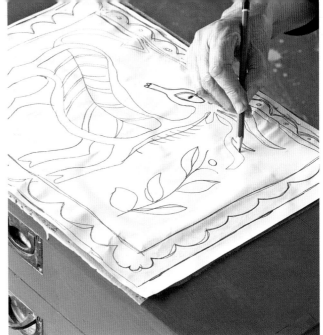

5 Divide your design into four sections and work on each of these individually, peeling back the paper and checking that the image has imprinted on the Duck Egg Blue paint underneath. Repeat all over the piece and then use the wax brush to apply clear wax once the paint is dry. Remove excess wax with a clean cloth.

CRACKLED LAMP BASE

For this wooden lamp base, I was inspired by *raku*, a type of Japanese pottery that's characterized by a fabulously crackled effect. This centuries-old technique was introduced to the West at the start of the 20th century and then became very popular in the 1950s and '60s. Whether ancient or modern, *raku* has a timeless quality. I love *raku* pieces in pale colors, such as natural creams and whites, as well as all the celadon, jade, and turquoise colors, which are usually cracked with dark black cracks.

Here I created a paintwork and crackle-varnish technique, but I reversed the tones and used Graphite with the cracks picked out in white wax. The technique involves applying two layers of paint, which are then sanded smooth and treated with crackle varnish. Although I did not slavishly copy a *raku* piece, I tried to recreate the chance way the pottery glaze dribbles down the side of a pot. *Raku* can be a springboard for many pieces, including pale colors with black wax to bring out the crackled effect.

YOU WILL NEED

- Chalk Paint® in Florence, Château Grey, Duck Egg Blue, and Graphite
- Small oval bristle brush
- Medium-grade sandpaper
- Annie Sloan Craqueleur Steps 1 and 2
- Small flat brush
- Hairdryer (optional)
- White wax
- 2 small wax brushes
- Clean, dry, lint-free cloths
- Clear wax

1 Use the oval bristle brush to paint irregularly shaped patches of Florence, Château Grey, and Duck Egg Blue over the base of the lamp. Dab and paint until the paint on the brush is more or less used up and then move on to the next color, using the same brush so that the colors blend well together.

2 Paint some areas more thickly and raised than others, even allowing drips to form, as these will show up later and are important at this stage. Allow to dry thoroughly.

3 Apply a thin coat of Graphite all over the base, making sure the first coat of paint is fully covered. Allow to dry.

4 Gently sand the Graphite with the sandpaper, taking off some of the Graphite to reveal the colors underneath. Flatten off any areas of uneven paint to make them smooth.

5 Apply Step 1 of the craqueleur with the flat brush, making certain you apply it all over, as any missed areas will not crackle. It will look white when first applied, but then dry completely clear. Dry with a hairdryer if you want to speed up the process, as it takes approximately 20 minutes to dry.

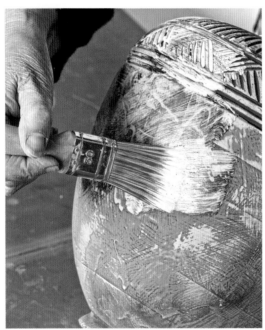

6 Apply Step 2 of the craqueleur, which is quite sticky and thick in consistency, and make sure you cover the whole area—you need to be very systematic in your application because it can be hard to see where you have been. Apply the craqueleur more thickly in some areas to create larger cracks. Either allow the base to dry naturally, in a warm, sunny environment, or use a hairdryer (make sure you do not hold this too close to the surface). This should take no longer than 5 minutes. The heat will make cracks appear.

7 Use one of the wax brushes to apply white wax quite generously all over the base, making certain that you apply it in all the cracks by brushing in all directions. Leave the wax on until it hardens slightly.

8 Wipe off the excess white wax with a cloth, taking off as much as you can while leaving the wax in the cracks.

9 To get a very clean look, use the other wax brush to apply clear wax to erase any undesired white wax from the surface, but leave the white wax in the cracks. Carefully remove excess wax with a clean cloth.

GILDED SOFA

I bought this French-style sofa at an auction and wanted to do something a little adventurous with it.

I was keen to use one of my Coloured Linens for the upholstery and to make something of the fringing. The sofa was covered and a large cushion made with my Louis Blue & Graphite linen. A separate trim was made using the Emperor's Silk and Aubusson fringing from two of my other fabrics.

With this powerful-looking upholstery I needed an equally striking design for the sofa's wooden surround. I love the very respectable and traditional history of gilding, but it also has a very daring aspect. Traditionally, the base color for gilding would be Primer Red, an earthy red-brown color, so I decided to beef it all up and use the bright red from my paint range, which is called Emperor's Silk.

To make as much of the red as possible, I applied bleach to the brass leaf and then wiped it away to reveal the red. I also waited for the gold to darken and oxidize, and go a little verdigris-blue-green in places. The finished effect is a little outrageous, but definitely out of the ordinary.

YOU WILL NEED

- Chalk Paint® in Emperor's Silk
- 2 small flat brushes
- Fine-grade sandpaper
- Water-based gold size
- Talcum powder
- Loose brass leaf
- Stencil brush
- Latex (rubber) gloves
- Thick household bleach
- Clean, dry, lint-free cloths
- Clear wax
- Small wax brush

1 Use one of the flat brushes to paint the wooden surround of the sofa with Emperor's Silk, making sure that the carvings are all covered. Once the paint has dried, ensure the surface of the wood is smooth by going over it with the sandpaper. This is essential because the brass leaf is very fine and will show up any bumps and brush marks.

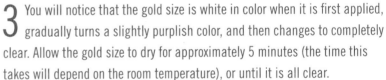

2 Gold size is a special type of glue for metal leaf that remains sticky for many months. Use the other flat brush to apply gold size all over the sofa surround.

3 You will notice that the gold size is white in color when it is first applied, gradually turns a slightly purplish color, and then changes to completely clear. Allow the gold size to dry for approximately 5 minutes (the time this takes will depend on the room temperature), or until it is all clear.

4 Dust a little talcum powder on your hands to help you handle the brass leaf. It will adhere to anything that is slightly sticky— even to your hands! Let the brass leaf drop onto the area, aiming for the deepest recesses. Use the stencil brush to dab the leaf gently into all the intricate carvings. Make sure you don't stroke the leaf, as it doesn't bend and might break into small pieces.

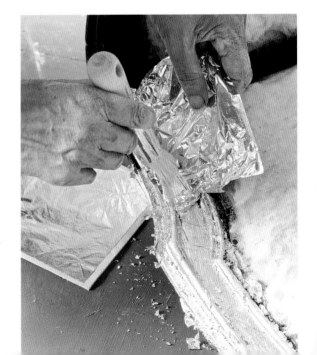

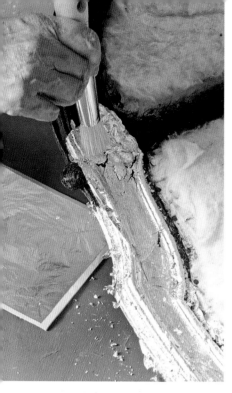

5 Overlap the brass leaf when placing it on the piece so that it joins well at the seams and there are no gaps. The leaf may break and split in some areas, so go over these with another piece of leaf.

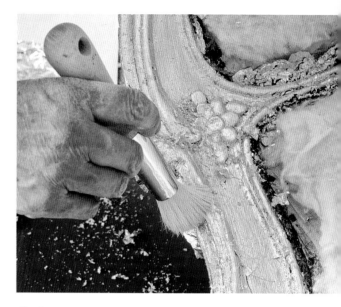

6 Once the whole area is covered with leaf, remove the excess by brushing/pushing it away. If you find that you have missed a few places, just apply more gold size followed by more brass leaf. At this stage the effect won't look great, but don't worry about that.

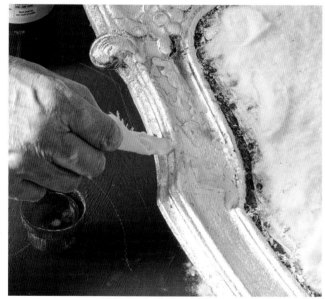

7 Carefully pour some bleach into the lid of the bottle and dip a piece of cloth into it. Take care with the bleach to protect yourself and your clothes— you may want to wear latex (rubber) gloves. Drop small amounts of bleach onto the brass leaf. The bleach will react and tarnish the metal by darkening it; the extent to which this happens will depend on the environment and the temperature.

8 Heavy drops of bleach will act very quickly and leave very dark spots, while lighter dabs with the cloth will create a deeper gold-bronze color. If you leave the bleach on overnight, or for a day or so, blue-green verdigris spots will begin to show.

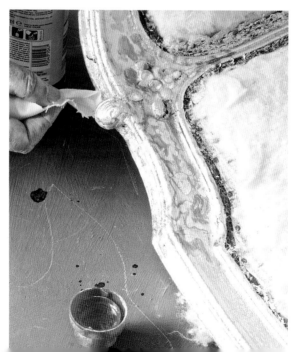

9 While the bleach is still wet, wipe away some of the brass leaf to reveal the red paint underneath and then dab the area dry with a cloth to stop the bleach continuing to work. When you are happy with the effect, leave overnight to dry and then apply clear wax the next day.

10 Apply the clear wax with the wax brush, doing this gently to avoid brushing away the verdigris marks. The wax will prevent any further tarnishing, as brass tarnishes naturally in the atmosphere over time.

11 Brush the wax every which way to ensure the piece is fully coated and remove excess wax with a clean cloth. Leave the piece until the next day if you want to buff it to achieve a polished shiny look. Even though the piece has been waxed, bleach will still work on the surface if you decide you would like more reaction.

Note: For instructions on making decorative fringing, visit www.anniesloan.com/techniques.

BRUSH-SHAPE PATTERNS

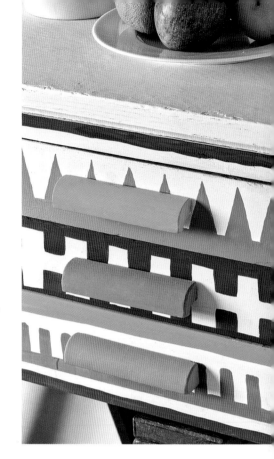

Felix and I talked about making patterns using brushes and came up with this idea together. Making geometric designs with brushes presents a challenge, as most people are not used to this technique; the temptation is to draw the patterns and then fill them in with paint. However, the quick method is to begin the whole process with brushes that then help to dictate the patterns you make.

There are lots of different brush shapes, but these come down to two basic shapes: pointed and square-ended. Everything has been done using only the brushes and paint. I also measured everything by eye—even my initial sketch. This piece of furniture keeps the lines straight and the overall design square, so small changes in the width give the piece a natural appeal.

YOU WILL NEED

- Chalk Paint® in Old White, Greek Blue, Primer Red, Antibes Green, and Scandinavian Pink
- Large flat brush
- Artists' pointed detail brush
- Artists' small, flat-ended detail brush
- Artists' medium, flat-ended detail brush
- Clear wax
- Small wax brush
- Clean, dry, lint-free cloths

1 Remove all the drawer handles before you start. Paint the piece all over with Old White first and allow to dry. Load the flat brush with Greek Blue, taking off the excess by wiping the brush gently on the edge of the can or basin. Then move the brush down the side of the drawer at a steady, but reasonably speedy, pace to make a band of color. This type of brush is ideal, as it holds a lot of paint and allows you to move quickly through the job. Repeat for all of the straight bands of color on each of the drawers, including the border in Primer Red around the whole piece and the extra line of Antibes Green at the top of the lower drawer.

2 Take the pointed artists' brush and load it with Greek Blue, testing to see that the paint is flowing well. Add more water if it isn't. Hold the brush point at the height you want your triangle to be, then drop it onto the surface and immediately pull down, adding more weight as you go. Straighten the sides to make the angles of the triangle. Each triangle will need a fresh dip of paint.

3 Take the small, flat-ended artists' brush and load it with Scandinavian Pink, again testing to check that it isn't holding too much paint. Decide on the height and then pull down to create columns of color.

4 Use the wider of the two flat-ended artists' brushes in the same way as the other marks to make short, wide rectangles in Primer Red at the top and bottom of the drawer, resulting in an H-shape on the Old White. Replace the drawer handles and then paint them in three of the colors you used, but in contrast to the drawer color. Apply clear wax with the wax brush and remove excess wax with a clean cloth.

STENCILED AND HAND-PAINTED CHEST OF DRAWERS

Throughout history, stenciling has been used to paint a repeat design that looks as if it is hand-painted and is still used today to create a measured repeated pattern. In contrast, this stenciled chest of drawers has been made to look unique. I was inspired by one of my stockists to combine seemingly random stenciling and hand-painting. To begin with I was more or less copying. However, hand-painting allows your distinctive style and character to come through, so let yourself approach this project in your own way, because each person uses a brush differently. This is a project for anyone who loves to paint and is prepared to give it a go. Although the stencils appear to be placed randomly, they are, in fact, applied in a balanced way, with more or less space between them in different places. The cool, solid base of pattern is brought together with flashes of warm color that give the piece movement and pizzazz.

YOU WILL NEED

- Chalk Paint® in Provence and Old White

- Small project pots of Chalk Paint® in: Napoleonic Blue, Antibes Green, Burgundy, and Barcelona Orange

- Annie Sloan MixMat™

- Small sponge roller

- Annie Sloan Oak Leaves stencil

- Artists' pointed detail brushes

- Clear wax

- Small wax brush

- Clean, dry, lint-free cloths

1 I made a paint mix for the base color of the chest of drawers because I wanted to create a paler blue color by mixing Provence and Old White. I used my MixMat™ to work out the ratio of the colors—here I used 10½ fl oz (300ml) of Provence to 3½ fl oz (100ml) of Old White paint. I then used this ratio to make up a larger quantity of paint. Stir well and use the sponge roller to paint the base color on the piece of furniture, in this case a chest of drawers. Allow to dry.

TIP

Although I painted this chest of drawers on its side, it is much easier to lay it on its back when stenciling. Remove all the handles before you start, so that you have a flat surface to work on.

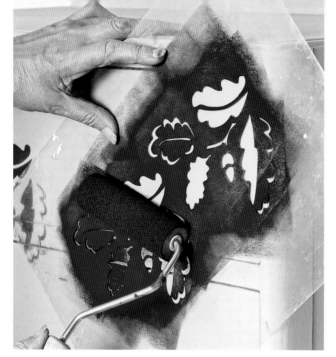

2 Use the MixMat™ to roll out some Napoleonic Blue, then stencil the Oak Leaves design randomly onto the piece. Hold the stencil firmly with your hand to stop it moving.

3 Place the stencil in different directions and leave some gaps in the arrangement as you stencil for the other colors.

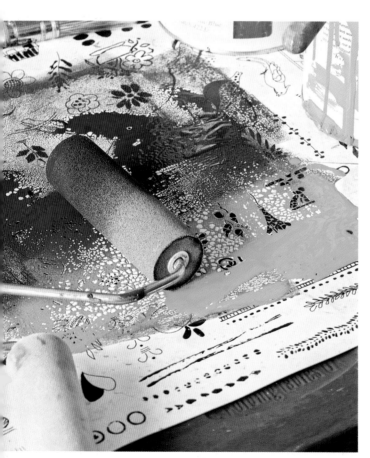

4 Add some Antibes Green to the MixMat™ and combine it with the Napoleonic Blue. Load the roller with paint (combining both of the colors) and start to stencil, gradually adding more Antibes Green until you only have Antibes Green left on the roller.

5 Use the roller to stencil those areas that do not have any blue stenciling with the Antibes Green.

6 Overprint some of the stencils so that the Antibes Green stenciling covers the Napoleonic Blue in some places.

7 Using various artists' brushes, free paint in some small details by following the outline of a leaf, filling in an acorn, or echoing a shape with a flowing line. I used the warm bright colors of Burgundy and Barcelona Orange to act as a contrast to the cool blues and greens. Finally, use the wax brush to apply the wax. Remove excess wax with a clean cloth.

PAINTERLY DINING ROOM TABLE

This is the Victorian table in my dining room, which is painted and waxed in Emperor's Silk. I wanted the table's colors to echo that of the walls. We have had it since our children were little, so it is much loved. It has been through many transformations, as I've searched for the perfect design. Originally in the kitchen, it is now used less often, so I felt I could do something more "demanding." I painted it in a series of mainly gray-greens, as well as some cool neutrals, with Antibes Green and a little Florence acting as a contrast to the bright red. I cut the design into four equal parts and organized these to achieve an interesting arrangement of shape and color.

I also wanted the table to be painterly, a word often used by artists to describe a style in which the paintwork is loose and expressive, rather than confined within drawn lines. Paint is, after all, what I am about, and it's my table and quite central to me. The finished design changed little from my original small painting, but I did mix some Antibes Green into the Graphite. I also added cool blue-green Florence, as I needed to balance the grayness and yellowness of the greens against the red.

YOU WILL NEED

- Chalk Paint® in Emperor's Silk, Château Grey, Antibes Green, French Linen, Graphite, Paris Grey, and Florence
- Sketchbook
- Scissors
- Pencil, for marking out the table
- Small and large oval bristle brushes
- Annie Sloan MixMat™
- Clear wax
- Small wax brush
- Clean, dry, lint-free cloths

1 Do a little painting in your sketchbook first, using the Emperor's Silk as your ground color and then adding a series of borders like the paths in a maze.

2 Once you have come up with a pleasing design, photocopy it and then cut it into quarters, as shown.

3 Arrange the pieces in a way you feel is the most interesting and balanced. In my design, I wanted to be sure that the Graphite was evenly balanced across the piece.

4 Paint the top of the table in Emperor's Silk and let dry. Very lightly mark out the four quarters of the table and then set about painting each one. It is easy to get lost, so I found it helpful to refer to the old and the new designs as I worked. As you paint, be aware of the red shapes as much as possible because they are as important as the green ones.

5 Use big brushes to paint the lines, be bold with your marks, and, when you mix the colors on the MixMat™, make sure that a little of another color gets into the mix. Take care not to over brush to make a shape "perfect." Instead, try to get the brush loaded with the right amount of paint, be sure about where you are going to paint, and do this confidently.

6 In places, where you want slabs of different colors to meet, scrub the wet paint into existing wet paint edges so that the colors merge softly.

7 Florence is a slightly brighter green than the gray greens and should be blended in so that it's hardly visible. To do this, dip the side of the brush in the Florence, so there is only a tiny amount of paint on the brush. Once the paint is dry, use the wax brush to apply clear wax very thoroughly all over. Use a clean cloth to remove excess wax.

WAREHOUSE RUSTIC

I sometimes come across really old, beaten-up pieces of furniture, particularly chests of drawers, which have layers of paint that often finish with a modern, brightly painted color. They look as if someone has tried to scrape off the colored paint, but given up halfway through, revealing all the layers underneath. I really appreciate these "chance" layers, random markings, and hints of other colors in places.

This is quite different to the subtle, worn look of old painted pieces in muted colors. It is a much more robust and rugged look in clear colors. I find it particularly appealing when the colors are quite strong; perhaps it's a little to do with an appreciation of modern abstract painting.

This old, mahogany-veneer piece was in very bad shape and destined for furniture heaven because large areas of the veneer had chipped, cracked, and lifted. The piece also had gouges, a few cigarette stains, and missing moldings. It would once have been a lovely piece of furniture, but by lifting and cutting the veneer and using a little wood filler, it became paintable.

I developed this method by experimenting with the paint and using a combination of techniques, including brushwork, using bleach to weaken the paint, scraping, and waxing to create a great, warehouse, rustic patina.

YOU WILL NEED

- Chalk Paint® in Paris Grey, English Yellow, and Provence (optional)
- Large oval bristle brush
- Thick household bleach
- Clean, dry, lint-free cloths
- Latex (rubber) gloves
- Mixing stick
- Scraper
- Clear wax
- Wax brush
- Dark wax
- Black wax
- White wax

1 Leave the lid off the can of paint overnight so that it really thickens up. Use the large oval bristle brush to apply Paris Grey over the whole piece of furniture, very generously and in uneven layers. This stage may take some time to dry.

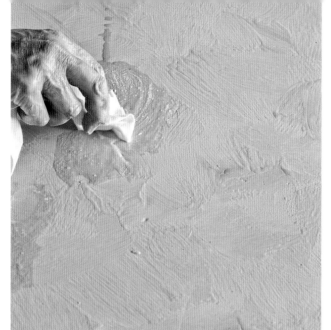

2 When the paint is dry, drop thick household bleach onto it in patches. If you wish, you can also use a clean cloth to apply the bleach to the paint. Take care with the bleach to protect yourself and your clothes—you may want to wear latex (rubber) gloves.

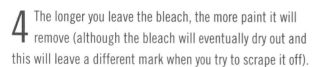

3 Dab a cloth on the wood to soak up some of the excess bleach. This will also remove some of the unwanted paint.

4 The longer you leave the bleach, the more paint it will remove (although the bleach will eventually dry out and this will leave a different mark when you try to scrape it off).

5 Using the end of the mixing stick, held at a 45-degree angle, gently scrape the surface, taking some of the paint away completely to reveal the layer of wood underneath. Pressing harder or softer will produce different marks.

6 Use the oval bristle brush to paint slabs of English Yellow on the piece, but leave some gaps. The paint should be thick, but try to use a light hand so that the paint sits on the surface. At this stage I also applied a little Provence in a few areas, such as the very base of the piece and the moldings.

7 While the paint is still wet, but starting to dry, use the edge of the mixing stick to scrape off some of the English Yellow, applying quite a lot of pressure in places. The more pressure you apply, the more paint will be removed. Then re-apply this thick wet paint by scraping it back onto the Paris Grey paint. This is a little like using a palette knife.

8 Use the scraper to get even further into the layers. This is particularly useful when the paint has dried, but not yet hardened.

9 Apply clear wax all over the piece and then remove any excess wax with a cloth. I then used dark and black waxes in places and, finally, white wax all over in parts to soften the effect of the darker waxes.

PAINTED CHANDELIER

I have a real soft spot for old brass lights such as these. This old French one has interesting classical details such as the triumphant, open-winged eagle at the top and the open-mouthed dolphin heads.

I knew that a coat of paint would transform it. I decided to keep it simple by just painting it and wiping away some areas of paint to highlight the shiny brass and the delicate and interesting detail.

I chose to paint the chandelier in a strong color because I like the ease with which it can add color and make a great statement in a room. I used Florence, a strong, coppery verdigris-green, which contrasts softly with the brass, but other strong colors such as Giverny, Greek Blue, Napoleonic Blue, and Old Violet would also look good. I love to see the contrast of warm golden shiny brass with the cool greens or matte blue paintwork.

YOU WILL NEED

- Chalk Paint® in Florence
- Medium oval bristle brush
- Piece of toweling or a sponge
- Clean, dry, lint-free cloths

1 Use the oval bristle brush to paint the chandelier all over with Florence, taking care that you get the paint into all the intricate areas. As these chandeliers can be very ornate, it's easy to miss parts, so I suggest you be very systematic—turn the piece upside down, so that you can paint all of the underside first, then paint it from above, and, finally, approach it from the side.

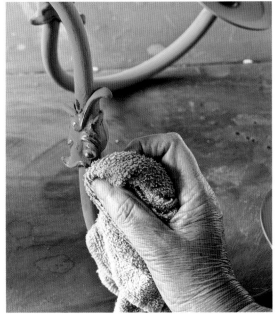

2 Once the chandelier is completely painted, take the absorbent piece of toweling or sponge and dampen it. Wipe away the paint from certain areas, especially on the raised details. Use a dry cloth to wipe off any excess wet paint. You may wish to wax the finished chandelier, but please note that the contrast between the matte Chalk Paint® and the shiny brass won't be as strong if you do this.

CHAPTER 2

FABRIC AND OTHER SURFACES

From drapes and sheer curtains to pillows and chair seats, plus a rug, a painted bowl, and an unusual shelf supported by painted rope, here is a whole host of inspiration to transform fabric and other materials that you may not have considered painting before, with some painted and dyed, some stenciled, and some printed.

PRINTED FOOTSTOOL

Printing using string, card, foam, lino, sponge, potatoes, and polystyrene (to name just a few of the things I've used on furniture and fabric) has always been one of my favorite ways of making pattern. Each item gives a slightly different paint print—the ones created by materials such as polystyrene and lino (see pages 14–17) are almost crisp, while those produced by sponge, for example, are soft-edged. I love the chance, uneven, and inconsistently printed result.

I used upholsterer's piping cord to print this footstool because it is soft and absorbs the paint well. I also like the broken-line effect created by the rolled cord. You could use string instead of cord, if you wish, although you may find some types of string have a coating that stops the paint adhering at all, which means the print will be unsatisfactory. So, test a few different types before you get going. The block is simply a discarded piece of wood that was left over after making some shelves.

You'll discover that printing on a colored fabric is better than printing on white fabric if you're using quite strong colors. The fabric used here is a mid-tone, neutral, textured natural linen. Play around with making various patterns and using different colors on paper or scraps of fabric before committing to a design. Use a generous piece of fabric, so that you can select the best printed area for your upholstery.

YOU WILL NEED

- Small project pots of Chalk Paint® in Emperor's Silk and Henrietta
- Wooden block
- Hot glue gun
- Upholsterer's piping or soft cord
- Annie Sloan MixMat™
- Small flat brush
- Annie Sloan Coloured Linen in French Linen & Old White
- Rag cloth
- Iron and ironing board

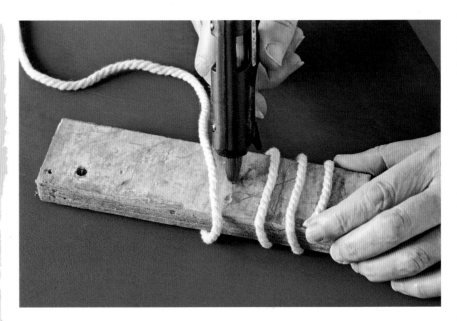

1 Take the wooden block and apply a couple of spots of hot glue to one end. Wrap the cord around the wood and, as you wrap, allow it to be both slanted and straight. Add more spots of hot glue as you wrap. Pay attention to each side of the wood, so that you can use both sides for printing. The slanting of the cord is part of the joy. (Although hot glue isn't essential, it does ensure that the cord doesn't slip out of place and smudge the paint.)

2 Working on the MixMat™, apply an even layer of Emperor's Silk to the cord with the flat brush. Before applying the paint to the fabric, check that the paint is even and printing well. The first prints are often a little uneven until the paint is properly absorbed by the cord.

3 Print rows of stripes in Emperor's Silk first, leaving gaps between rows that are wide enough for the rows in the second color of Henrietta. Keep printing until the fabric is covered with the striped design.

4 Wipe off the excess Emperor's Silk with the rag cloth and use the reverse side of the block for the Henrietta print.

5 Print the stripes in Henrietta in the gaps between the rows of red stripes. Once dry, iron the fabric to set the paint.

Note: For instructions on upholstering the footstool, visit www.anniesloan.com/techniques.

WAREHOUSE LEATHER CHAIR

This warehouse-style chair with leather upholstery needed a good clean before it was painted. Both the leather and metal were painted, transforming the chair. Most leathers and, indeed, some vinyl coverings are fine for painting, but a few have a finish that stops paint adhering. So, test a small patch before you paint a similar chair. Also bear in mind that squishy leather is more prone to folding and cracking than stretched leather. Any geometric design, such as arrows, circles, or lines, would be in keeping with the style. Use bright colors or very neutral, practical, machinery-like colors such as grays and blacks.

YOU WILL NEED

- Chalk Paint® in Emperor's Silk, English Yellow, and Graphite
  - Large flat brush
  - Masking tape
  - Small flat brush
  - Clear wax
  - Large wax brush
- Clean, dry, lint-free cloths (optional)

1 Use the large flat brush to paint the whole chair seat in Emperor's Silk, feathering out the paint as you work to achieve an even surface. (To feather out means to hold the brush at right angles to the work, lightly and speedily sweeping across the surface without over brushing.) Paint the back of the chair in English Yellow. Let the chair dry.

2 Using masking tape, mark out the stripe, bearing in mind that you will be painting the gap between the two pieces of tape. Make sure you stick the tape on straight.

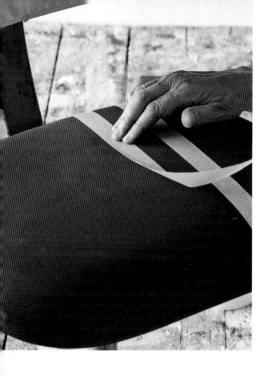

3 Paint the stripe in English Yellow with the small flat brush. You may need to apply two layers, or touch up where the coverage isn't completely even.

4 Carefully remove the tape as soon as the paint is dry or even before it's completely dry. If you leave the tape on for too long, you run the risk of removing the red paint underneath. When the paint is thoroughly dry, apply clear wax with the wax brush. For a high shine on the chair, buff the following day with a clean, dry, lint-free cloth. (I painted the metal parts of the chair in Graphite using the same brush.)

TIP

When using Emperor's Silk or one of the other reds in the Annie Sloan paint range, it's sometimes a good idea to use two coats of wax to seal the color thoroughly.

PRINTED PILLOW

I have several beautiful wooden printing blocks: some abstract-looking, rectangular, French ones, as well as several Indian blocks with an image of a tree or leaf, or a Paisley design. The aged patina of the wood makes them an interesting decoration for my home. Wooden blocks are a very old form of printing and can be found all over the world in various cultures. A piece of fine-grained wood is used, with the design being drawn on and then carved out of the wood. To ensure the wood doesn't warp, the block is quite thick, so it is pleasingly chunky. This printing method is still used in India and you can buy the blocks from craft fairs and specialist stores.

I have printed a pillow here, but the method could, of course, also be used to decorate some drapes (curtains), or perhaps a lampshade, table runner, or bed cover. Imagine a fine sheer drape printed with a delicate color! You will need a fabric that's not too coarse for your design. Really fine block designs have to be printed on a delicate fabric. More robust designs require a bit of texture in the fabric. Look at the smallest parts of the carving and compare them to the fabric weave. If the weave is bigger, the design won't show up clearly. I also advise printing onto a color, rather than onto white, so that the color and design of the print have something to connect to.

YOU WILL NEED

- Chalk Paint® in Aubusson Blue, Florence, and Old White

- Batting (wadding)—i.e. the type often used for quilting—or something equally soft, as the blocks are hard on the table and need something soft to press into

- Table protector (such as an oilcloth), to stop paint going onto and sticking to the table

- Medium-weave linen (enough to make the pillow, plus some extra to try out the design)

- Wooden printing blocks from India

- Small sponge roller

- Annie Sloan MixMat™

- Iron and ironing board

- Pillow pad, to fit the size of pillow

1 Cover the table with the batting (wadding) and table protector, ensuring the surface is soft, but firm. Put the fabric on the table. For this pillow, the fabric was dyed beforehand with Aubusson Blue (see pages 106 and 108 for advice on dyeing fabric). To make the pillow more interesting, I dyed the fabric for the reverse side in Florence and then printed the design in Old White.

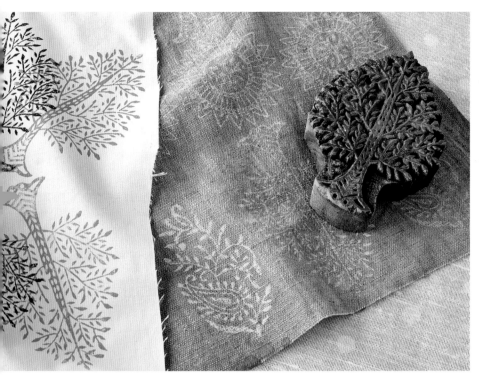

2 Experiment on a spare piece of fabric, making sure you know exactly how much pressure to apply and how much paint to use. The first one or two designs won't print as well until the paint has wet the wooden block sufficiently. Depending on the type of block, try printing the design in different ways, such as upside down or centrally, or perhaps alternate the design with a second block or print it in lines, etc. Be aware that printing on fabric is not going to give a perfectly even and consistent look, but this is part of its charm. Don't be discouraged if some of the pattern does not fully print when you start.

3 Apply the Old White paint to the printing block with the sponge roller, being careful not to get too much paint on the block. Work the roller on the MixMat™ to test beforehand.

TIP

Make sure you wash the wooden blocks thoroughly after use. Use a strong bristle brush such as a small flat brush to remove all the paint after printing and so prevent a build-up of paint.

4 Place the printing block on the fabric, checking that it is positioned correctly. Apply an even amount of pressure on the block so that the design prints consistently.

5 Iron the fabric on a warm setting to set the color. The fabric can be washed on a light wash, although you might lose a little of the strength of the color. I washed the dyed linen before printing on this piece of fabric, but haven't tried washing it after printing with the design.

6 Make up the pillow and insert the pillow pad before sewing up the last side. I left the Florence-dyed linen on the back of the pillow plain, but you can print the designs in Old White on this side too if you wish.

Note: For instructions on making up the pillow, visit www.anniesloan.com/techniques.

PAINTED ROPE SHELF

I made a wonderful rope swing in the garden for my granddaughter from thick rope and a chunky wooden seat. The rope went through holes in the seat, was securely knotted, and then frayed to make wonderful tails. I then dyed the tails with Chalk Paint® and they now remind me of a child's toy horse with a brightly colored mane.

So I took the idea further and came up with this shelf! It's the same basic idea--a chunky board threaded with two lengths of rope that are then knotted and frayed. Shelves are a constant issue for everyone and I think this is a great idea and a fun twist on the ordinary. I used rustic metal handles to attach the shelf to the wall and covered them with rope knotted like a braid, which I then painted too.

You'll need some natural-looking polyester rope, which is available from most hardware stores. Avoid nylon rope as this is shiny and slippery, and probably won't absorb paint. Polyester has an advantage in that it can be melted at the ends to stop it fraying. The rope can be frayed in different ways, depending on the material, either completely or leaving more defined strands, as I have. Painting the rope also offers several options. I did horizontal bands, which were painted before the rope was unraveled. These give a striped look all over, as some of the strands have paint on them and some don't. You could also paint each group of strands after unraveling the rope. Choose lots of colors or paint the rope all the same color. So, lots of possibilities!

YOU WILL NEED

- Small project pots of Chalk Paint® in: Barcelona Orange, Provence, and Olive
- Box of matches or a lighter
- Length of 3-strand, polyester rope, ⅓in (8mm) in diameter
- Small flat brush
- Fabric scissors or a sharp knife

1 Use a match or lighter to melt and seal the end of the rope, and so stop it fraying. Dilute the paint by dipping the brush in water before dipping it into the paint. Paint the rope end in Barcelona Orange and Provence, ensuring you get into all the grooves. I reversed the color blocks on each rope.

2 Allow the rope to dry thoroughly and then chop off the end with a strong pair of scissors or a strong knife. Tie a large, neat knot approximately 3in (8cm) from the end of the rope.

3 Twist the painted end of the rope in one direction to unravel it. This rope is made from three strands of cord, which I separated out, as shown.

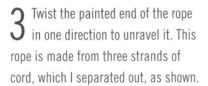

4 Unravel each cord further until you have separate "threads." I ended up with 12 separate threads, four from each cord.

5 Paint the knot above the "tails." I used Olive, which is a deep neutral color, to give the brightly colored tails more emphasis.

Note: For instructions on making the rope shelf, visit www.anniesloan.com/techniques.

PRINTED TABLE RUNNER

This is probably one of the easiest projects in the book! It is simply a piece of fringed fabric printed with a little paint using objects from my toolbox. What could be easier? However, the skill lies in finding a good piece of fabric of the right weight and keeping the design simple and uncomplicated. For this piece I used my Annie Sloan Coloured Linen in Old White and Old Violet. This has a tumbled look and a pronounced texture that matches the slightly unpredictable nature of the printing. The little dots and circles are quite delicate and restrained in contrast. The color chosen is also important, so the contrast is not too great.

I had fun raiding my toolbox for objects to make circular shapes, including a piece from a drape (curtain) pole, a rawl plug, and an assortment of nails and screws—all perfect for making dots, rings, and spots. So, choose to make rectangles, lines, squares, or triangles, and find suitable things for printing. I made a series of printed lines along the width of the runner, marking them randomly and irregularly. One of the joys of hand-printing is the way you can make an apparently repeated pattern look quite irregular! So some of the lines are made from many dots and others from just a few larger circles. If you are new to printing, then keep the design simple and use just one or maybe two colors.

YOU WILL NEED

- Chalk Paint® in Emperor's Silk
- Annie Sloan Coloured Linen in Old White & Old Violet
- Small flat brush
- Annie Sloan MixMat™
- Selection of circular objects, such as rawl plugs, nails, screws, bolts, and pencils, for printing
- Batting (wadding)—i.e. the type often used for quilting—or something similarly soft to press into
- Table protector (such as an oilcloth), to stop paint going onto and sticking to the table
- Iron and ironing board

1 I am not a lover of measuring things, but it's important to find the approximate center of the runner so that you can keep the design well balanced and the lines straight. My simple method involves folding the runner in half and then in half again. Continue folding in this way until you have the desired number of sections. Press firmly to make a fold mark in the fabric—this will give you guidelines for your design.

2 Brush a small amount of Emperor's Silk onto the MixMat™. The mat allows you to mix paints and can then be easily washed and used again.

3 Take your printing objects—I started with a fairly bold rawl plug, since it was not the biggest nor smallest of the pieces. Test the piece by dipping it in the paint and printing a couple of times on the MixMat™ to check that it has enough paint on it and is leaving a complete print.

4 Print the circular shapes on the fabric. Using the soft batting (wadding) and table protector beneath the fabric helps enormously to get a good print, as you need something soft for the fabric to sink into as the hard metal prints.

5 I then chose the end of a screw because it was the next size down, printing onto the fabric and using the fold as a guideline to keep the line of printed dots straight. I worked along the crease.

6 I then used the largest of the circle-making devices to ensure that the design was balanced, and continued making the lines.

7 Dip the pencil into the paint and place small dots in the center of some of the circles to give some variety to the repeated dots. Once dry, iron the fabric to set the paint. Wash as necessary on a low temperature.

Note: For instructions on making up the table runner, visit www.anniesloan.com/techniques.

SHIBORI LAMPSHADE

Shibori is the ancient Japanese art of dyeing fabric to make patterns. There are many ways to do this, from simply folding and dipping (as I have here) to more complicated methods. There is always a random element to the result, but you will learn to control your design to an extent. Once you start, you won't want to stop, as results are easily achieved. Use cotton sheet fabric to practice, but use good-quality fabrics such as fine linens and cottons with a good texture for finished pieces. Silk is also a possibility, since it's the traditional fabric often used in Japan. The fabric should not be too thick, as this will make it difficult to fold and it won't absorb the dye well. It will also be more difficult to make the lampshade because this involves folding the fabric tightly. Most of my paint colors work well, although I have found Napoleonic Blue and Aubusson Blue to be especially good. This may be because they're similar to the traditional color used in Japan. Off-white fabrics work well with the blue.

YOU WILL NEED

- Small project pot of Chalk Paint® in Napoleonic Blue
- A generous piece of vintage linen
- Large glass bowl
- Pitcher of water
- Mixing stick
- Iron and ironing board

1 Put approximately one tablespoon of Napoleonic Blue into the glass bowl.

2 Pour in the water and use the mixing stick to stir well, making sure the paint isn't sitting at the bottom of the bowl. Do a test patch on some spare fabric to check the color and add more paint if you need to make it stronger.

3 Concertina the fabric by folding one way, turning the fabric over, then folding the fabric back on itself. The bigger the fold, the bolder the pattern will be.

4 Concertina-fold the fabric again, but this time into triangles.

5 Fold and then turn the fabric over and fold on the other side. Repeat until you have a complete triangle and tuck in any loose edges.

6 Before you dip the fabric, make sure the paint has not settled at the bottom of the bowl. If it has, then stir again to mix. Dip the first edge of the folded fabric in the dye and hold for a second until the dye seeps into the fabric. You need to keep the center of the fabric white. Note that the paint mix will continue to absorb a little after you take out the fabric.

7 Repeat this step for the other two sides of the triangle. Make sure there is still some undyed fabric left in the center, otherwise there will be little or no pattern.

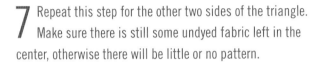

8 Open up the fabric immediately to see the pattern and hang it up to dry. You can keep the piece of fabric folded, but it will take much longer to dry like this. Once dry, iron the fabric on a warm setting to set the color.

Note: For instructions on making up the lampshade, visit www.anniesloan. com/techniques.

DYED LACE SHEER CURTAIN

I found this single panel of quite intricate, machine-made, cotton lace in a box of old sheer curtains in a house clearance store. This one caught my eye as a good target for dyeing because it had a beautiful pattern, but it was very grubby and had several stain marks.

You will need a container such as a basin, old pail (bucket), or bath tub that can hold enough water to cover the piece of fabric you are dyeing. The fabric also needs space to move around in the water. If the container is too small, there is a risk that the dyeing will be patchy and uneven.

This is such a simple technique, but take care when choosing the color for the dye and also consider the fabric and original color of the piece you're using. For example, I found that this piece of cotton dyed very easily. However, although I've found most synthetic sheer fabrics also dye well, some may have a finish that stops them absorbing color completely. To be sure, test a small piece of the fabric first before embarking on dyeing the whole piece.

This fabric was already a muted, toned-down, "dirty" white. If I'd wanted to dye it a bright color, I wouldn't have been successful. To achieve this, I would have needed a really white fabric to start with. Also, if I had chosen a brightly colored fabric at the outset, the end result would have been muted—this might have looked good, but could just have easily looked a little dirty. For this reason, I chose a dark, muted paint color—in this case, Graphite—which created a dark charcoal color that obliterated the stains and gave the fabric a wonderful silhouette against the light of the window.

YOU WILL NEED

- Chalk Paint® in Graphite
- Old pail (bucket) or bath tub
- Water
- Tablespoon
- Mixing stick
- Old lace sheer curtain (net curtain)
- Iron and ironing board (optional)

1 Fill the pail (bucket) or bath tub with enough water to cover the fabric well, and then add a spoonful of the Graphite paint. I added a tablespoon of paint, but paint colors are not all the same strength, and you should consider the weight of your fabric, too, so I suggest using a smaller amount of paint to begin with, then adding more as needed to achieve the desired strength. Use the mixing stick to mix in the paint, making sure that it is completely dissolved. I like to use my hands to do this, so that I can search for any clumps of paint.

2 Dunk a little of the sheer curtain into the dye to test the strength of the color. If you're happy with the color, immerse the curtain fully and soak it for a few minutes, making sure that all the fabric is covered with the dye. Again, I like to use my hands to work the dye through the fabric to ensure the whole piece is covered.

TIP

If the color is too strong or too weak, you can either re-dye the piece or wash it in a washing machine to take out some of the color.

3 Remove the curtain from the dye and allow it to drip dry. Heat the curtain to seal in the color, either by putting it in a tumble dryer, ironing it, or hanging it in hot sun.

Note: For instructions on making up the sheer curtain, visit www.anniesloan.com/techniques.

PAINTED UPHOLSTERED CHAIR SEATS

How many chairs have you seen in perfect condition, but with upholstery fabric that's not to your taste? Lots, I'm sure. Here is a method for painting the fabric and wood to transform the piece. It's difficult to give precise measurements for the ratio of paint to water, as each piece of upholstery is different—the fabric may be thick, textured, and not too absorbent or thin and very absorbent. The upholstery may be made from traditional horsehair or newer batting. So, bear these golden rules in mind. Use more water, rather than too much paint. Only apply one or two coats. Think of the process as staining, not painting. Let the fabric dry before applying another coat. Use a paint color that covers the fabric underneath—it is hard to cover a dark pattern with light pastels and whites.

YOU WILL NEED

- Chalk Paint® in Old Violet and Château Grey
- Medium oval bristle brush
- Clean, dry, lint-free cloths
- Small flat brush
- Piece of paper

1 Dilute the Old Violet with some water first because the paint needs to flow easily, be quite easy to apply, and offer no resistance. Apply the paint with the oval bristle brush, making sure you start with a wet brush and then move quickly to cover the fabric.

2 Some areas of the fabric may not cover well at first, so go back into these wet areas with a little more paint. Always keep the brush wet—don't use pure paint. Also try not to overpaint and soak the chair. Continue until you have finished painting the whole chair seat and don't stop halfway through the job.

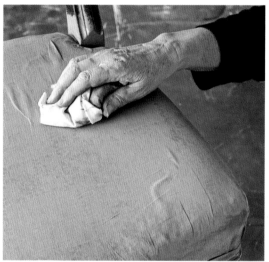

3 Now that the paint is solid and even, take a cloth and wipe off the excess. This may expose the pattern in the fabric. If you don't want this to happen, allow the fabric to dry and re-paint it once more. The fabric will stretch a little because it's wet. Don't worry, as it will shrink back again when dry.

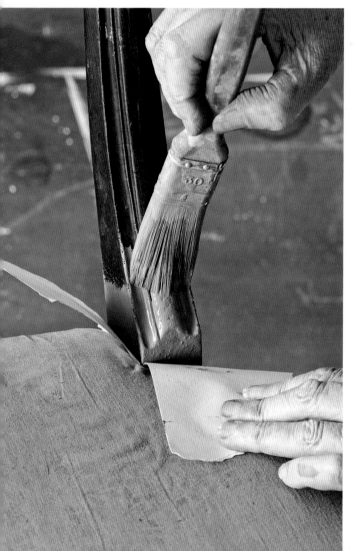

4 I chose to paint the fabric first and then the wood in Château Grey afterward, but you can paint the wood first if you wish. In either case, take care not to damage the already painted area. To avoid getting paint on the painted upholstery, rather than using masking tape, just tuck a piece of paper into the crevice between the wood and the upholstery. This method is for unwaxed upholstery and I painted this chair with the intention of not waxing, to achieve a soft natural look. If you do apply wax, then the effect will be more like leather than a stained fabric.

TIP

If you would like the fabric pattern to show through, add more water when applying the paint. Alternatively, you can apply two coats with a little water so that the pattern is obliterated. If you apply too much paint, then the surface may be too hard and perhaps even rough. If this does happen, sand the chair seat with sandpaper.

FOLDED AND TIED PAINTED FABRIC

This technique is inspired by *shibori* in that it involves folded and tied fabric but, instead of dipping the fabric in a paint mix, I simply painted it with diluted paint. The trick is to use a good-quality and, ideally, heavy fabric such as this vintage linen. The lighter and thinner the fabric, the more paint the fabric absorbs, but I like to use a slightly thicker fabric so the paint does not spread so wildly. Do not make folds in regular stripes, as it's the irregularity of the stripes at slight angles that gives the design its interest. I did this pillow in a blue-green mix, as I am inspired by the Japanese *shibori* of blue on white (see the Shibori Lampshade on pages 102–105), but I love the other combinations shown here too, where Primer Red has been used on fabrics dyed with my paint colors, such as Graphite with Antibes Green, and French Linen and Florence with Primer Red. This is an elegant and more restrained approach to tie-dyeing than the sunbursts of color of the swinging '60s and psychedelic '70s and would fit into any interior.

YOU WILL NEED

- Small project pots of Chalk Paint® in Florence and Aubusson Blue
- Vintage linen
- Fine string, cut into approximately 8in (20cm) lengths
- Scissors
- Large flat brush
- Iron and ironing board

1 Gather the fabric into the center from top to bottom until your thumb and finger meet in the middle. Don't try to make the folds too even, but allow them to differ in height and size.

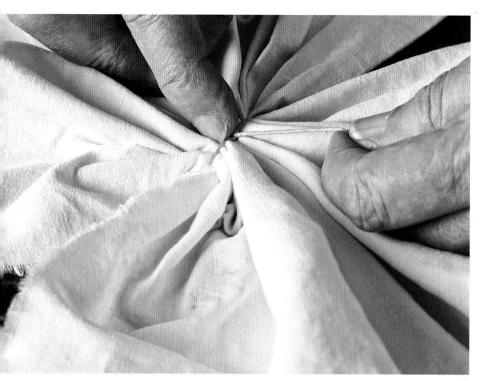

2 Holding the gathered fabric with one hand, use the other hand to tie a length of string around the gather and knot it as tightly as you can.

3 Gather the fabric and tie it again, with approximately 3-in (8-cm) gaps between each tie, until you reach the end. I made four ties in my piece of fabric.

4 Use the flat brush to moisten the folds with some water—the fabric needs to be quite moist, but not fully saturated. The dryer areas will not absorb as much paint as the wet areas.

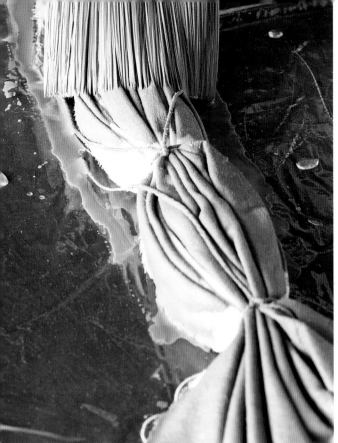

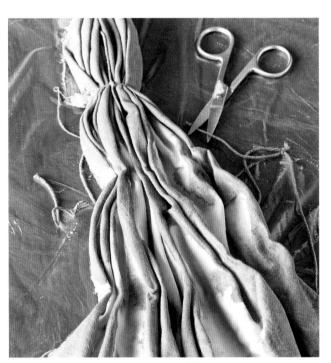

5 Make a paint mix using the Florence and Aubusson Blue. Use the flat brush to brush the paint mix onto one side of the piece of fabric only. Use a light touch so that the paint doesn't go too deeply into the folds. No extra water is necessary in the paint mix, as long as the paint can be painted on easily, because there is already water on the fabric.

6 Allow the fabric to sit for approximately 5 minutes, then use the pair of scissors to cut the string ties.

7 Carefully open out the piece of fabric to see the pattern and then leave to air-dry. Once dry, iron on a warm setting to set the color.

Note: For instructions on making up the pillow, visit www.anniesloan.com/techniques.

DYED DUST SHEET

Finding four dust sheets online for a ridiculously small amount of money—each one being about the price of an expensive coffee—sparked the idea for these drapes (curtains). When they arrived, I realized that they really were "dust" sheets for covering furniture during building work, rather than heavy, closely woven pieces of fabric for providing protection when painting. These dust sheets are made from light, 100-percent cotton fabric, with an open weave, which results in slightly sheer drapes that allow light to come through. If you wish, you could line the drapes or double up the fabric to make them opaque.

The dust sheet fabric was a little yellow, so I had to take this into consideration when selecting the colors. If I had used a blue dye, the result may have been a little green. I chose Scandinavian Pink, which dyed the yellowish fabric a light peachy color. The color was a little too strong, so I washed the fabric immediately before sealing it with heat. This took out some of the color, creating a pretty, delicate pink. The washing, drying, and ironing changed the dust sheet, shrinking the fabric and turning the fabric from smooth to one a little like cheesecloth, with a great texture.

For the stenciling, I used Scandinavian Pink again and Château Grey—a warm color with a cool muted gray. I only chose one stencil design and found that using a stencil brush to apply the paint, rather than a sponge roller, was more successful on this fabric. The trick with the stenciling was to know when to stop! A little goes a long way and it's essential to leave some areas free of any pattern.

YOU WILL NEED

- Chalk Paint® in Scandinavian Pink and Château Grey
  - Old bath tub
  - Water
  - Tablespoon
  - Mixing stick
  - Dust sheet
- Iron and ironing board
- Annie Sloan Sand Dollar stencil
  - Stencil brush

1 Pour enough water into the bath tub to cover the fabric well and then add a tablespoon of the Scandinavian Pink paint (see step 1 on page 106 for advice on how much paint to use for dyeing). Remember to consider the type of fabric you are using—this one is a little transparent with a loose weave and also rather yellow. Mix the paint well into the water. You can use a mixing stick to do this, but I like to use my hands to give everything a good stir, as the paint will settle at the bottom of the bath tub.

2 Dunk or dip the dust sheet in the dye. The paint may resist a little at first, so make sure you really work it into the fabric.

3 Keep working the fabric, making sure you don't miss any areas. If you think the fabric looks too dark, then rinse it out a little to remove some of the color. Washing the fabric will really soften it and this particular piece actually shrank by about 20 percent, so bear this in mind if you are measuring up for a pair of drapes (curtains). Dry and iron the fabric before starting the stenciling.

4 Practice stenciling on a piece of spare fabric first before attempting the whole piece, to gauge the strength of the color and the amount of paint needed on the stencil brush.

5 Randomly position the Sand Dollar stencil on the dust sheet and use the brush to stencil the whole of the design in either the Château Grey or Scandinavian Pink.

6 I worked back and forth across the fabric with the two paint colors, randomly placing the designs in a cluster and sometimes filling in only the center of the stencil to make a small "flower." After I had dyed and stenciled my dust sheets, I made them up into drapes.

Note: For instructions on making the dust sheets into drapes, visit www. anniesloan.com/techniques.

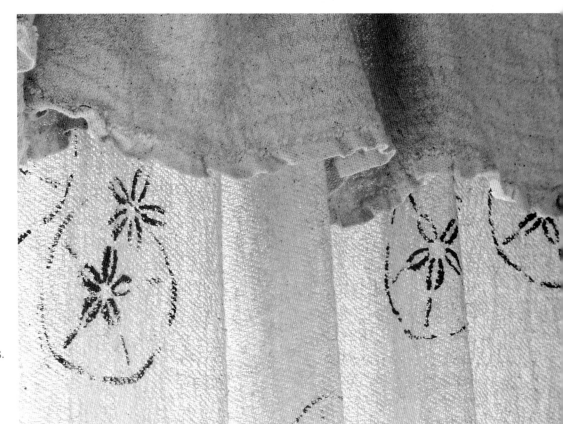

PAINTED GLASS BOWL

When I decided to write a book called *Annie Sloan Paints Everything*, I thought that I must really paint everything! I have included furniture of all sorts and finishes, rope, fabric of all types, and metal, but I needed another kind of surface. Then I remembered the glass bowls I painted many years ago, so this is a reworking of that idea. I have always loved painting these. It is very easy to do and achievable by anyone.

Painting bowls first started because I once needed a bowl for mixing paint in my studio, having run out of places and being too lazy to wash up. I found a bowl in my kitchen cabinet, thinking it would be easy to wash. In fact, it would have been easy to wash if I had done it straight away, but I left it too long and the paint set and became very hard. However, I noticed how beautiful the paint looked though the glass, and so an idea was born.

In this design, I have kept everything very simple by choosing a set of blues with one light warm green, Versailles, by way of gentle contrast. I chose colors that are mid-tone—with white added to the Aubusson Blue and Napoleonic Blue—as they give better coverage. My design is very free and I wasn't aiming for perfection.

YOU WILL NEED

- Small project pots of Chalk Paint® in: Greek Blue, Provence, Aubusson Blue (with a little Old White added), Napoleonic Blue (with a little Old White added), and Versailles
- Glass bowl
- 5 small flat brushes
- Clear varnish

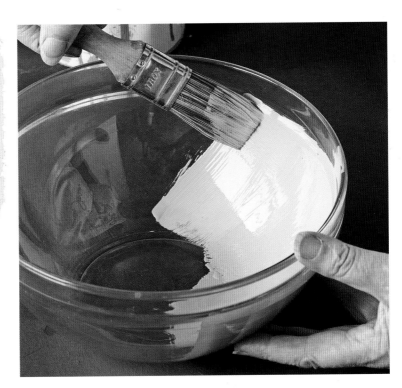

1 Using one of the brushes, paint a fairly generous section of Greek Blue, which is a mid-tone color, on the inside of the bowl, without pressing too hard on the glass—or apply two layers to get a good coverage. While this first section is still wet, use another brush to apply a darker color next to it (here I used Provence), but in a narrow stripe. Don't worry if you leave any gaps.

2 Continue adding stripes in the other colors, using a clean brush each time, until the whole inner surface of the bowl is painted, including the base.

3 Using the handle of a brush, scratch lines into the wet paint. This step can be done once the paint is almost dry or when it's wet. Vary the width and frequency of the lines.

4 Paint and cover the inside of the bowl in the Versailles paint. Once the paint has dried thoroughly, apply varnish with a clean flat brush.

WASHED-OUT STRIPED DRAPES

These unusual patchwork drapes (curtains) came about by chance after making table runners decorated with strips of paint for a big dinner party for our stockists. I made them with other people, and some people applied the paint thickly, some very sparingly, while others made the paint more watery.

After the party, I washed the strips on a low temperature and noticed how the paint had washed out partly and unevenly, depending on how it had been applied in the first place. The result was really attractive. I wondered how I could use these wonderful strips and then came up with the idea of sewing them together with the raw edges showing. I chose a natural linen fabric, because this has a wonderful texture. It also has a neutral color which means it works well with all the paint colors. The finished drapes are very pleasing and all the better for being a combined effort by many people who had never painted before.

YOU WILL NEED

- Chalk Paint® in Primer Red
- Other Chalk Paint® colors of your choice (I used Greek Blue, Château Grey, and Aubusson Blue)
- Strips of Natural Linen (the width of my fabric strips range from 14½–19in/37–49cm, but they are all approximately 98in/250cm in length)
- Masking tape
- Tape measure
- Small oval bristle brush
- Iron and ironing board

1 Cut strips of fabric in the same or different widths—the one shown here is 14½in (37cm) wide. Lay two strips of masking tape down a central line, so that the strip to be painted is 5in (13cm) in from the edge and around 2in (5.5cm) wide. Make sure the tape is straight and stuck on firmly.

2 Use the oval bristle brush to apply the Primer Red quite solidly, but not thickly. Don't add water to the paint, as this will make it seep under the tape. Allow to dry thoroughly. Repeat with the other colors on the other strips of fabric.

3 Pull the tape off each drape (curtain) and then heat them by pressing with a hot iron or put them through a tumble dryer. Wash the drapes at a low temperature to take off some of the paint, so the fabric is soft and the paint uneven.

Note: For instructions on making up the drapes, visit www.anniesloan.com/techniques.

SWEDISH PAINTED BLIND

I was inspired to make this blind after staying in a friend's traditional Swedish barn. I drew a picture of it so I could make similar blinds for my house and studio. My friend's windows were lower, smaller, and shorter than mine, so it was easy to reach up and release the fabric from the hooks. My blinds probably won't get much use, because they are too high to be unhooked easily, but I like the way the blind looks at the top of the window. My blinds are also wider, so there is a soft dip in the fabric that was less apparent in the Swedish ones.

YOU WILL NEED

- Chalk Paint® in Aubusson Blue
- Annie Sloan Coloured Linen in English Yellow & Antibes Green
- Large table, for painting the stripes
- Tape measure
- Masking tape
- Small flat brush
- Iron and ironing board

1 Measure the blind to find out where you want the stripes to be. Apply masking tape to the fabric to mark out the two thin side stripes. Press the tape firmly onto the fabric to ensure that no paint will seep under the tape. It's really important to test the paint's characteristics on a piece of scrap fabric between some strips of tape before starting. The paint must be a little dry, with only a small amount of paint on the brush. Do not load your brush with lots of wet paint or, again, it will seep under the tape. Paint all the thin stripes on the blind and then remove the strips of tape, starting with the first ones, which should now be dry.

2 Apply the tape in the same way to make the wider stripes on the fabric, making sure you achieve the same paint quality as before.

3 The paint will dry very quickly, so pull off the strips of tape as soon as it is dry. Then iron the fabric to seal it. I washed the fabric gently by hand, but this could also be done in a washing machine on a cool, gentle wash. Washing the fabric takes away any paint hardness and softens the whole look.

Note: For instructions on making up the blind, visit www.anniesloan.com/techniques.

STENCILED RUG

I have made several burlap (hessian) rugs and love the way they remain very soft and pliable even when covered with paint. I made this piece of burlap into a rug by taking two layers of fabric and then folding over and sewing the edges to make a wide border. This not only gave the rug strength, but also meant the border could be used for the black design.

I experimented with different designs using several stencils on spare bits of burlap. I "measured" everything by eye, and then filled in any areas that looked a little bare. I am inspired by traditional Persian carpets, where colors are changed and some parts of the design missed out—these imperfections give a rug life.

YOU WILL NEED

- Chalk Paint® in Graphite
- Burlap (hessian) fabric
- Small flat brush
- Annie Sloan MixMat™
- Small sponge roller
- Annie Sloan stencils: Bell Flowers, Valeska, Classical Bird, and Sand Dollar
- Iron and ironing board

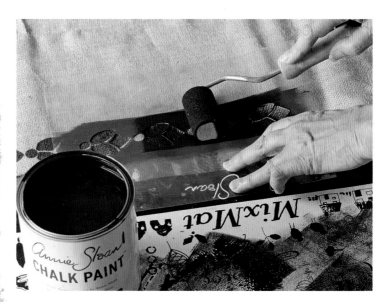

1 Transfer some Graphite to the MixMat™ using the flat brush. Load the dry roller with paint, making sure it is not too full by testing it on a spare piece of burlap (hessian). If the roller is too wet, the paint will spill out under the stencil. You'll also need to try out the roller a few times on some spare fabric to get it sufficiently immersed in paint to work successfully—that is, not too wet and not too dry. A small amount of paint goes a long way. Position the Bell Flowers stencil on the burlap and apply the paint lightly at first, then with more pressure. For the second print, line up the last flower with the previous print by eye to ensure the gaps are the same.

2 Position the Valeska stencil next to the Bell Flower. Start in the center of the rug, and continue stenciling. These stencil designs don't match perfectly in length, so don't worry when you see the V-shape of the Valeska stencil meeting the Bell Flowers in different places as you move along.

Note: For instructions on making up the burlap rug, visit www.anniesloan.com/techniques.

3 Position the Classical Bird stencil and calculate visually how many birds will fit along the length of your rug. There were a few gaps at the ends and corners of my rug, so I filled these by stenciling in the little branches from the bird stencil. I finished by stenciling another line of Bell Flowers on the inside of the rug and filled the outermost corners with the Sand Dollar stencil. Once dry, I ironed the rug with a hot iron to seal the paint, but I did not varnish or protect it in any other way.

ALPHABET TRANSFER BANNER

Sometimes, you see old blinds in secondhand stores or when you move into a new home, and wonder what you can do with them, because they never fit anywhere apart from the place they were intended for. This is a brilliant solution. The blind shown here was made into a banner with a simple transfer design. Felix had made an alphabet banner for his daughter, so we came up with a method to make something similar.

For an alphabet, you will need space for 26 letters in seven rows, with four letters in five of the rows and two lines with three letters. If you find measuring stressful, either get someone to help you—as I did—or do a more irregular placing of the letters. I found an alphabet free of copyright that I could print out. You will need to print the letters reversed (as a mirror image), so that they are not backwards once transferred.

It is important to take your time to do this project well. Allow the paint and the paper cutouts to dry thoroughly for several hours, or overnight. If you don't, then the paint can rub off too easily and the printed ink can smudge and run.

YOU WILL NEED

- Chalk Paint® in Provence, English Yellow, Antoinette, and Greek Blue
- Old blind
- Scissors
- Pencil
- Yardstick (meter ruler)
- Medium oval bristle brush
- Small flat brush
- Reversed alphabet letters (see Introduction above), printed on ordinary computer printer paper
- Annie Sloan Découpage Glue and Varnish
- Clean, dry, lint-free cloths
- Clear wax
- Small wax brush

1 Cut the top and bottom off the blind so that you have one piece of fabric. Place the blind on your work surface with the fabric side facing uppermost.

2 Draw lines lightly in pencil on the blind, measuring carefully with the yardstick (meter ruler) so that you have a line going though the center of each letter. I marked a spot on the line where each circle of color would be.

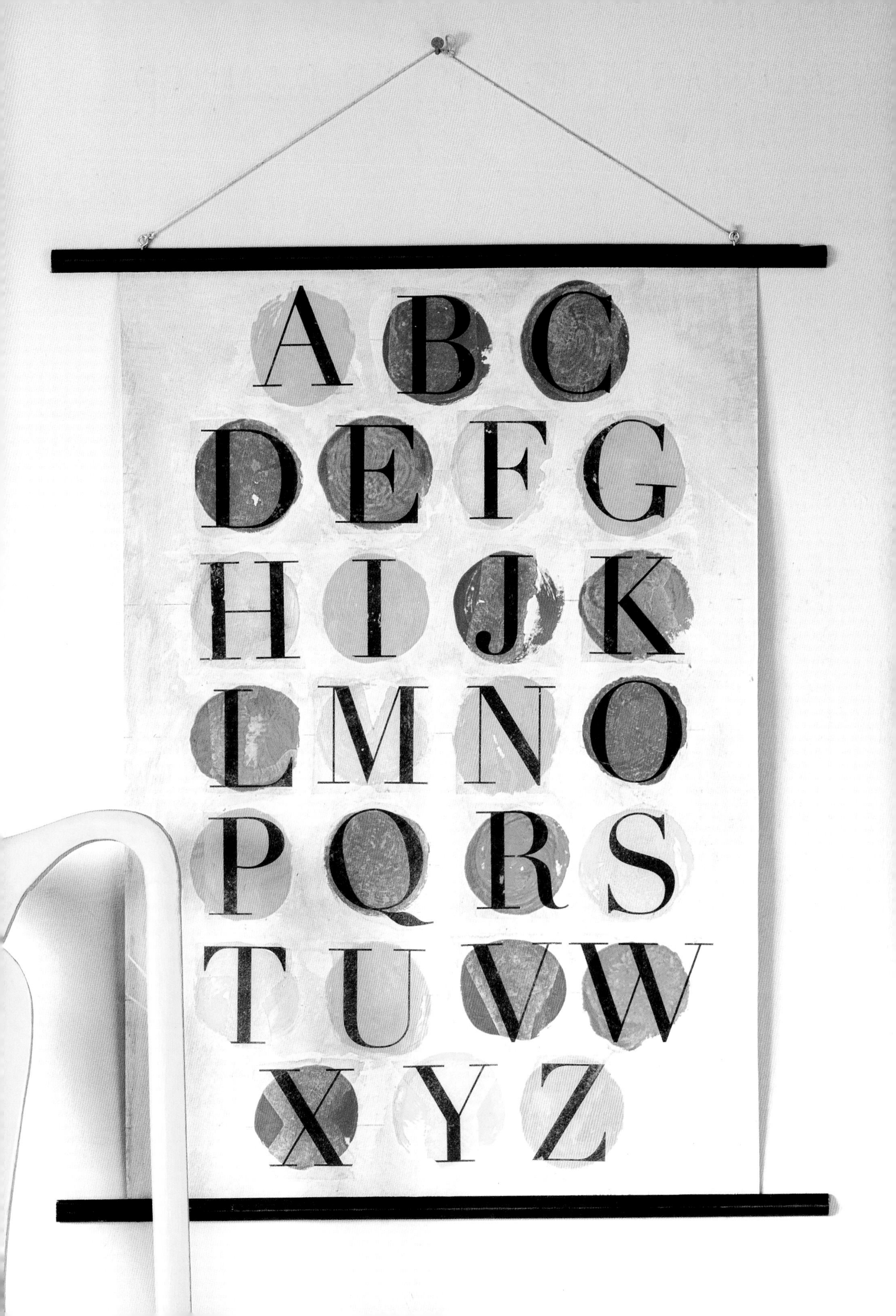
A B C
D E F G
H I J K
L M N O
P Q R S
T U V W
X Y Z

3 I chose four colors and then used the oval bristle brush to paint each one with a swirling twist to give a bit of movement to the shape.

4 Roughly cut out the letters in whatever way you want, bearing in mind that the more paper you leave on the pieces, the more you will have to remove later.

5 With the print side facing upward, use the flat brush to coat the first letter transfer with découpage glue.

6 Stick the transfer immediately on its painted spot. Let dry thoroughly for several hours at least. Repeat for each of the letters.

Note: For instructions on making up the banner, visit www.anniesloan.com/techniques.

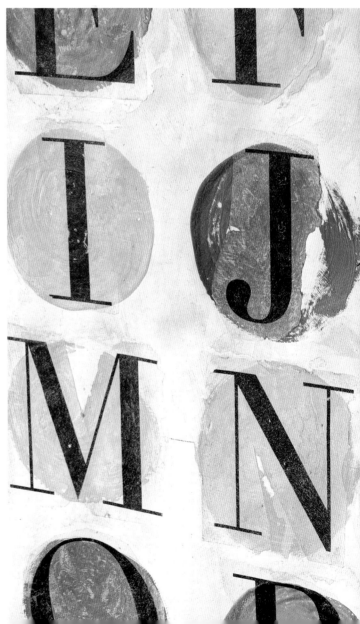

7 Soak the transfers with some water using your finger, rubbing at the same time to remove the paper. Use a cloth to help you remove the paper and allow to dry. You may need to take off more paper because, as it dries, you will find that the paper is still very white in places and less so in others. If the paper is still white and solid, then remove this by adding more water. Some parts might break and split. Bear in mind that some of the paper will disappear when you wax the finished banner. Apply clear wax with the wax brush and remove excess wax with a clean cloth.

CHAPTER 3

WALLS AND FLOORS

Give character to your home with these classic modern looks that include simple paint and wax, floral stenciling, and richly textured walls. Go for a sharply contemporary feel with brightly colored frottage, or something more subdued with waxed rustic planks. There's also a parquet floor with a great washed effect.

RANDOM STENCIL WALL

This type of stenciling is the most fun to do, as it allows you lots of freedom. There is basically no measuring and you can place the stencils anywhere you wish. However, although it may look as though I simply "went for it," there are, in fact, some guidelines and imposed restrictions to follow that will help make your random stenciling work really well.

The key thing is to restrict the colors you work with. I mainly worked with blues but, most importantly, these were three blues of different tones. I have the mid-tone-colored blue of Giverny for the background and deep-colored Napoleonic Blue and pale Louis Blue for the stenciling. To go with these, I chose Barcelona Orange, which is the complementary color to blue. Some of the stencil colors are mixed, which makes it look as if there are more colors than there really are. By working on a mid-tone background color, you can go darker and lighter with the stenciling, thus giving your work depth immediately. In contrast, the small amount of very warm orange, tempered a little with Louis Blue, gives the design some lift.

I chose four of my Annie Sloan stencils, which varied in size and type. These stencils included one side of the large but quite detailed and trailing Antheia, which were all done in the blues. The rest of the stencils were flowers: a bold spot (using the middle section of Petrushka) with the similar stems of Arctic Poppy and the tiny, daisy-like flowers of Flower String. Try to keep some space between the stencils, with nothing else on the wall, to give it lightness; otherwise the wall will look too dense and heavy.

YOU WILL NEED

- Chalk Paint® in Giverny, Napoleonic Blue, Louis Blue, and Barcelona Orange

- Annie Sloan MixMat™

- Large stencil roller

- Annie Sloan stencils: Antheia, Petrushka, Arctic Poppy, and Flower String

- Medium oval bristle brush

- Masking tape

- Small stencil roller

1 Paint the wall in Giverny and make sure it's completely dry before you start. Then place the Napoleonic Blue on the MixMat™ and roll out the color with the large roller.

Antheia

Arctic Poppy

Flower String

Petrushka

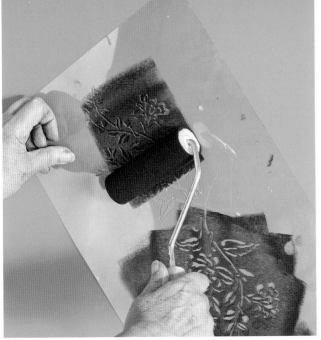

2 Place the first stencil randomly on the wall, ensuring that there is enough paint on the roller to stencil several times. (I only used half of the Antheia stencil here and applied about 16 stencils with the one roller of paint.)

3 Position the stencil at different angles each time, with lots of space in between the prints in order to vary the pattern slightly.

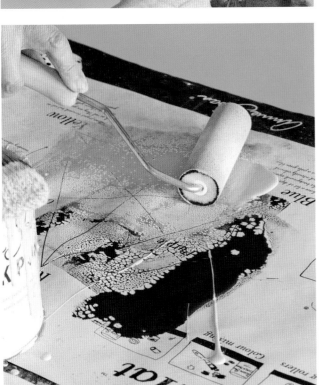

4 Use the oval bristle brush to put some Louis Blue on the MixMat™ and load the roller with paint, combining both the colors to create a mid-tone paint. Don't worry if the paint isn't mixed in.

5 Position the stencil on the wall again, overprinting the first stencil in Napoleonic Blue with the Louis Blue.

6 Take into consideration the direction and shapes of the previous stencils, so that you give the design some dynamics.

7 Load the roller with paint again, this time adding more Louis Blue to the mix to create a lighter shade, so that you now have stencils in three colors on the wall, but using only two paint colors.

8 Take the Petrushka stencil and tape over the parts that you don't want to use. You could make a paper cutout if you prefer. Repeat for the Arctic Poppy and Flower String stencils.

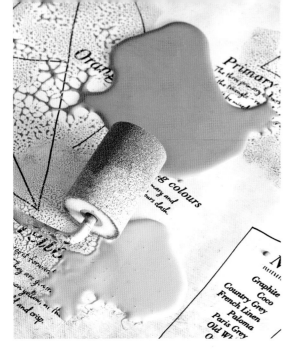

9 Put a dollop of Louis Blue and Barcelona Orange on the MixMat™ (having cleaned the other paint from it thoroughly first).

10 Load the small roller with a combination of Barcelona Orange and Louis Blue, and print the flowers from the Petrushka, Arctic Poppy, and Flower String stencils on the wall.

EMPEROR'S SILK WAXED WALL

One of my favorite looks and finishes is a wall that has been painted and waxed. I have this finish on my dining room wall in the same rich red and I have created the look in Graphite in my house in France, too. I've also seen it done in Old White and polished with an electric buffer to within an inch of its life. Stunning! I'm sure, given the right context, that any color would look good on a wall with this treatment. My walls have been done with a cloth to achieve a soft sheen, but I can certainly see the appeal of the highly polished look. It's a matter of style. The rich sheen of the wax on the very absorbent Chalk Paint® has such a soft and mellow look. The very shiny look is ultra modern and sleek.

This idea is very simple to do; although it is not the quickest of looks to achieve, the end result is so rewarding. The initial layer of paint needs to be applied well, so that there is a good mixture of evenly and unevenly applied brushstrokes. These should not be too apparent, although a few give the wall a gentle texture that's very appealing.

YOU WILL NEED

- Chalk Paint® in Emperor's Silk
- Large oval bristle brush
- Clear wax
- Large wax brush
- Clean, dry, lint-free cloths
- Electric buffer (optional)

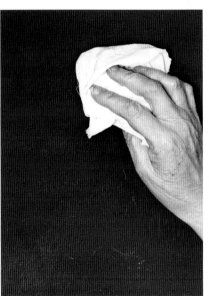

1 Paint the wall with Emperor's Silk using the large oval bristle brush, feathering out the paint. Bear in mind that any texture will show up when you wax, so apply the paint quite smoothly—although a little texture is quite acceptable and, in fact, desirable to give the wall some character. Allow the wall to dry completely. Apply a generous amount of clear wax in stages using the wax brush, wiping off the excess as you go along.

2 The next day, polish the wall with a clean cloth to give a sheen. If you want a super sheen, then you can use an electric buffer.

WASHED WOOD

I first came across the idea for this richly textured finish when I made a table out of two wooden pallets, one on top of the other. I use the table in the design rooms at the warehouse where we all work in Oxford, England. Unfinished pallet wood is just too raw and plain for us "sophisticated" people in design! Plus, of course, it also has a texture that is rather too rough for comfort. So I came up with a finish which is a little different to my normal method. Usually, I apply paint and then wax it afterward, but this time I reversed the process! The result is rich and textural, yet smooth and characterful.

Since then I've used this method on various walls, notably in my rustic bathroom in my house in France. There I used a ragtag of old used boards, both planed and unplaned, and even scaffolding boards too. I was able to unite them all with the rich, textural finish of dark wax and Old White paint. If you wanted a little more color on the wood, the colors and their combinations could easily be varied, so try using black wax, instead of the dark wax, and overlaying it with Duck Egg Blue or Paris Grey, for instance.

YOU WILL NEED

- Chalk Paint® in Old White
- Dark wax
- 2 large wax brushes
- Large oval bristle brush
- Clear wax
- Clean, dry, lint-free cloths

1 Use one of the wax brushes to apply dark wax generously into and over the area of wood, making certain you cover it all. The wood may absorb a lot of the wax, depending on the type of wood you are waxing, so ensure the dark wax remains sticky and isn't all absorbed into the wood. It's essential to apply the wax in strips, so that the wax stays wet/fresh for the next step.

2 Create a wash with the Old White by adding water to the paint, making sure it is quite watery and runs easily over the still "wet" wax, while still remaining opaque. Use the oval bristle brush to paint the wash over the dark wax without working it in too much—just make sure that there are no drip marks.

3 Once the paint and the dark wax are dry, use the other wax brush to apply clear wax to seal the wood completely. Remove excess wax with a dry cloth.

PARIS GREY PARQUET

Parquet is a very old form of flooring that uses small, usually rectangular, blocks of wood, which are pieced together like a mosaic to form a simple pattern. It became very popular in the 1950s and '60s, and is now returning to popularity as people find reclaimed parquet flooring and re-lay it in their houses.

Finding evenly colored parquet flooring in perfect condition is not easy, as I discovered with this particular parquet. The warmth of the wood can also be unappealing for people who prefer a cool color as a backdrop to their rooms. After finding, cleaning up, and laying this old floor, I found it was, indeed, rather too yellowish, as well as too uneven in color and stained in places.

I was able to even out the differences with a wash of one color. A wash of paint means diluting the paint with water until it is translucent, so allowing the wood grain to show through. The paint wash can be as dilute as you wish, but you should test the strength of the color after you have applied the lacquer. This is because the application of lacquer reduces the opacity of the wash, so you may need to make the wash slightly more opaque to achieve your desired finished effect. Each floor will be different, so do a test patch before you begin, particularly with the final lacquer as this can draw out brown or yellow stains from the wood. If this happens, then an application of clear shellac is necessary before you begin.

I chose to do a wash of Paris Grey over the wood before lacquering it. Other paint-wash colors that would work well over the wood are Graphite, one of the whites, or Duck Egg Blue.

YOU WILL NEED

- Chalk Paint® in Paris Grey
- Pail (bucket)
- Large sponge
- Large flat brush
- Clean, dry, lint-free cloths
- Lacquer
- Large sponge roller

1 Test the color of the Paris Grey wash with the lacquer over it on a small piece of spare wood (see Introduction above). When you are happy with the mix of paint and water, make a pail (bucket) of the mix and apply with the sponge, wiping and rubbing it all over the floor. When applying the paint mix, you need to be quick and decisive, and work on the floor in sections.

2 After using the sponge to apply the paint, you may find that you need to spread the paint so that it is even. This will depend on the absorbency of the wood.

3 Use the flat brush to get into the edges and corners of the room.

4 To get an even effect on the floor, rub off any excess with a clean, dry cloth.

5 Stir the lacquer well before using a large sponge roller to apply it all over the floor. Using a sponge roller ensures you have a thin coat. Use a flat brush to reach the edges, again applying only a thin coat. Once dry, apply a second coat of lacquer in the same way.

FABRIC WALL

This wall is covered with burlap (hessian), an adaptable and economical fabric that you can purchase in quite wide quantities. My main inspiration was seeing something similar, with batons and a simple molding, in the attic of an English historic house. The idea for painting the burlap came from the popularity of colored burlap when I was first decorating in the 1970s. So, I combined these ideas to line the wall with burlap, adding painted batons and some beautiful old molding for the cornice. I padded out the burlap with two layers of batting (wadding) to make the wall feel soft, although this means the fabric absorbed a lot of the paint mixture. For me, the finished result has a comforting, glamorous, retro look, which combines the textured country style of painted burlap with the soft warm opulence of the gold.

YOU WILL NEED

- Chalk Paint® in Olive and Duck Egg Blue

- Burlap (hessian) and batting (wadding), enough of each to cover your wall

- Staple gun, to attach the burlap (hessian) to the wall

- Large oval bristle brush

- Lengths of old cornice (if necessary)

- Half-round wooden dowels, for the batons

- Hammer and tacks

- Masking tape

- Annie Sloan Warm Gold Gilding Wax

- Artists' brush

1 I fixed the burlap (hessian) and batting (wadding) to the wall with a staple gun, and then painted and tacked the dowels and cornicing into place afterward. Take the oval bristle brush and wet it before you start. It is essential to add water to the paint so that it will flow freely on the burlap, and yet remain opaque. If the brush isn't flowing on the burlap, your paint is too thick and you will need to add some water. If some areas of paint are too solid, then brush them out with a wet brush. I made my paint-and-water mix (using the Olive paint) as I went along, which meant my wall was not completely even as I worked back into the paint. If you want the surface to have an even layer of paint (and be a consistent color), make a large amount of paint-and-water mix and then apply it without going over an area twice.

2 My wall had no cornicing, so I used some reclaimed old cornice. Paint the lengths of cornice with Duck Egg Blue mixed with a little Olive. Paint the half-round dowels with the Duck Egg Blue and then tack these to the wall at regular intervals, leaving space at the top for the cornice to be added later (if necessary).

3 Before applying the gilding wax, mask out any areas that you don't want to cover in wax. I like to apply the gilding wax with my finger, as it's quite sensitive to the shape.

4 Use the artists' brush for those areas that are hard to reach with a finger. Tack the cornice in place over the burlap wall (if necessary).

Note: For instructions on attaching burlap and batting to a wall, visit www.anniesloan.com/techniques.

FROTTAGE WALL

Frottage is a way of adding a random texture to walls or furniture, and is basically achieved by applying runny paint and then flattening crumpled-up newspaper over the chosen surface to create texture.

It's fairly easy to do, but you need to be well prepared before starting, with plenty of scrunched-up newspaper ready to use and also plenty of translucent paint mix so that you don't run out of paint halfway—this is particularly important when you are using a paint mix. You need to work quickly and may have to add a little water as you go along. Check the absorbency of the wall with a test patch first—walls that have been painted many times will be less absorbent than new walls with fewer coats on them. You will have to work very quickly on a new wall.

The results of this technique can look very different depending on the colors. I've done it before in very muted colors such as Château Grey over Duck Egg Blue or Versailles over French Linen, and the effects were very much faded luxury and grandeur, a little reminiscent of marble. For a different effect, use Antibes Green underneath and Napoleonic Blue on top, or Antibes Green over English Yellow, as I have here. The effect is immediately very contemporary.

YOU WILL NEED

- Chalk Paint® in English Yellow, Antibes Green, Provence, and Old White
- Large oval bristle brush
- Old newspapers

1 Paint the wall in English Yellow and allow to dry. To make the paint wash, mix equal quantities of Antibes Green and Provence, adding a little Old White to soften the color. Dilute this paint mix with water until you achieve the translucency you would like. Use the wash to paint an area about 4in (10cm) larger than a sheet of the newspaper in the top left corner of the wall. You should still be able to see the yellow color underneath.

2 Scrunch up a sheet of newspaper, open it out, and then press the paper onto the wall, smoothing out the sheet and leaving borders approximately 3–4in (8–10cm) wide on the right and below so that you can work back into them. Peel back and discard the newspaper. Don't leave the paper on the wall for too long or it may begin to stick.

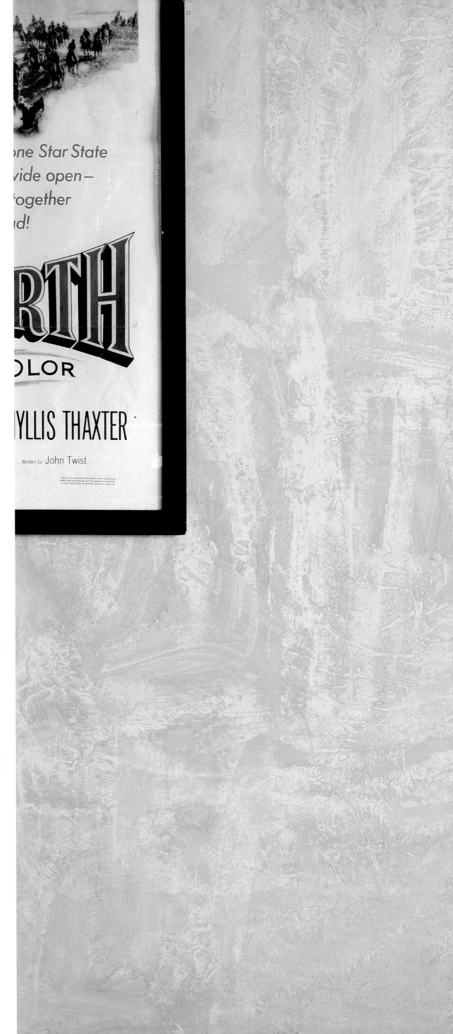

3 Work back into the already applied
paint, which should not have dried yet.

4 Repeat the newspaper process as
above until the wall is covered.

ROUGH AND LUXURIOUS WALL

This wall finish appeals to me greatly, reminding me of the uncertain charm of old walls that are stripped and pared back to show remnants of old wallpapers and paint layers— hinting at a possibly rather grand or intriguing history. Combined and contrasted with luxurious architecture or furniture, this look is always a winner.

To give the wall depth and interest, I worked with three basic paint tones, building on the warm and neutral color of Old Ochre. I used mid-tone blues on this as my main color with a little of the warmth and depth of Coco in parts. I finished with Old White as my lightest tone.

This project will take time and care, and it can't be hurried. I like to apply the paint with a piece of cardboard because this is soft and doesn't make scratchy marks, and yet is still firm to hold. However, it absorbs the paint after you have used it for 5 to 10 minutes and becomes too soft, so a fresh piece is needed. A piece of soft pliable latex (rubber) might work too, but I've not found one yet.

The final finish, using an electric buffer to polish the wall and give it a beautiful sheen, is best done only when the paintwork is really dry. Waxing as a final effect is simply for protection.

YOU WILL NEED

- Chalk Paint® in Old Ochre, Duck Egg Blue, Louis Blue, Coco, and Old White
- Sturdy cardboard boxes
- Annie Sloan MixMat™
- Coarse-grade sandpaper
- Electric buffer
- Clear wax
- Large wax brush
- Clean, dry, lint-free cloths

1 Paint the wall all over first with Old Ochre and allow to dry. Have a quantity of cardboard boxes cut up ready nearby. Pour more or less equal amounts of the mid-tone paints, Duck Egg Blue and Louis Blue, directly from the cans onto the MixMat™.

2 Take a piece of cardboard and scrape the two paints together, mixing the two blues roughly on the MixMat™ before applying the paint to the wall.

3 Softly scrape the paint along the wall, varying the pressure as you go. Apply the paint all over the wall, as this will be the main paint color with a paler blue over it.

4 Pour some Coco onto the MixMat™. It doesn't matter that you still have remnants of the previous paint mix on the mat.

5 Apply the Coco to the wall in the same way as the previous color, although at lower quantities because this is a dark color and will have more impact.

6 Pour the Old White onto the MixMat™ next and combine this with the blues and any leftover Coco to make a pale blue-grey color.

7 Apply a layer of this paint to the wall in the same way as before. Finally, apply Old White over the wall in places and allow to dry thoroughly.

8 Smooth with the sandpaper to remove any very uneven paint. Use an electric buffer to make the wall shine. You can finish the wall with clear wax applied with a wax brush to seal it. Remove excess wax with a clean cloth.

USEFUL ADDRESSES

Chalk Paint® is available throughout the UK, Europe, US, southern Africa, Middle East, Far East, Canada, Japan, Australia, and New Zealand. For a complete list of stockists where you can buy Chalk Paint® and my other products, please go to www.anniesloan.com.

Please note that the swatches shown in the color wheel on page 9 are only a representation of the paints. To obtain a hand-painted color card, please find your local stockist on the Annie Sloan website. Each color card contains our entire range of colors.

Follow me on:
Blog anniesloanpaintandcolour.blogspot.co.uk
Facebook facebook.com/AnnieSloanHome
Twitter twitter.com/AnnieSloanHome
Instagram instagram.com/AnnieSloanHome
Pinterest pinterest.com/AnnieSloanHome
YouTube youtube.com/AnnieSloanOfficial

PAINT COLORS AND MATERIALS USED

In many of the photographs in this book, not only are the projects decorated using Annie Sloan products, but so are the walls, floors, and furniture. Here are details on what was used from the Annie Sloan range.

Page 14 Lino-print Chair Wall: Versailles Wall Paint; skirting board: Chateau Grey Chalk Paint®; floor: Paris Grey Chalk Paint®.

Page 19 Textured Paint Radiogram Wall: Graphite Wall Paint; skirting board: Paris Grey Chalk Paint®; floor: Old White Chalk Paint® Wash and Dark Soft Wax.

Page 22 Reverse Stencil Folk Table Wall: Amsterdam Green Chalk Paint®; chair: Old Violet Chalk Paint®; floor: Dark Soft Wax.

Page 27 Smooth and Textured Cabinet Wall: Graphite Wall Paint; chair: Primer Red Chalk Paint®; pillow: Emperor's Silk & Florence and Louis Blue & Graphite Coloured Linens; floor: Château Grey Chalk Paint®; skirting board: Paris Grey Chalk Paint®.

Page 31 Tile-effect Stencil Table Wall: French Linen Wall Paint; chairs: Barcelona Orange and Provence Chalk Paint®; floor: Château Grey Chalk Paint®.

Page 34 White Wax Bureau Wall: English Yellow Chalk Paint®; skirting board and floor: Graphite Chalk Paint® Wash; chair: Louis Blue Chalk Paint®; letters: Olive and Old Violet Chalk Paint®.

Page 39 Making an Arc Wall: Graphite Wall Paint; chair: English Yellow Chalk Paint®; lamp base: Barcelona Orange Chalk Paint®; lampshade: Barcelona Orange & Napoleonic Blue Coloured Linen; lampshade buttons: Old White & Louis Blue Coloured Linen; floor: Château Grey Chalk Paint®.

Page 52 Wet Paint Drawing Wall: Aubusson Blue and Napoleonic Blue Chalk Paint®.

Page 57 Crackled Lamp Base Wall: Antibes Green and Florence Chalk Paint®, rolled with a sponge roller; lampshade: Aubusson & Provence Coloured Linen.

Page 60 Gilded Sofa Wall: Aubusson Blue with Napoleonic Blue Chalk Paint® brush work over it; skirting board: Graphite Chalk Paint® wash; floor: Dark Soft Wax.

Page 67 Brush-shape Patterns Wall: Old White Wall Paint; skirting board and floor: Old White Chalk Paint®; trestle legs and frame: Graphite Chalk Paint®.

Page 69 Stenciled and Hand-painted Chest of Drawers Wall and skirting board: Antoinette Wall Paint; floor: Old White Chalk Paint® with lacquer; lamp base: Barcelona Orange Chalk Paint® with Clear Soft Wax; lampshade: Barcelona Orange & Napoleonic Blue Coloured Linen.

Page 72 Painterly Dining Room Table Wall: Emperor's Silk Chalk Paint® and Clear Soft Wax (see page 142); bookshelves: Duck Egg Chalk Paint®; chairs: upholstered in English Yellow & Antibes Green, Emperor's Silk & Florence, Aubusson & Provence, Louis Blue & Graphite, and Emile & Graphite Coloured Linens.

Page 77 Warehouse Rustic Wall: Old White Wall Paint; skirting board and floor: Old White Chalk Paint®.

Page 85 Printed Footstool Wall: Paris Grey Wall Paint; drapes: Pure Linen dyed with Provence, Arles, and Florence Chalk Paint®.

Page 89 Warehouse Leather Chair Wall: Paris Grey Wall Paint; skirting board: Old White Chalk Paint®; floor: Dark Soft Wax.

Page 95 Painted Rope Shelf Wall: French Linen Wall Paint; shelf: Louis Blue Chalk Paint®.

Page 103 Shibori Lampshade Lamp base: Aubusson Blue Chalk Paint®.

Page 111 Painted Upholstered Chair Seats Wall: Louis Blue Chalk Paint®; skirting board: Château Grey Chalk Paint® with Clear Soft Wax.

Page 113 Folded and Tied Painted Fabric Wall: Emperor's Silk Chalk Paint®; floor Dark Soft Wax; sofa: Graphite Chalk Paint®, upholstered in Gentleman linen; pillow: Coco and Duck Egg Blue Coloured Linen and Primer Red Chalk Paint® shibori; Pure Linen and Florence Chalk Paint® shibori; vintage linen and Aubusson Blue shibori; vintage linen and Napoleonic Blue shibori; Pure Linen dyed with Florence Chalk Paint® and Primer Red stripes.

Page 120 Painted Glass Bowl Wall: Antibes Green Chalk Paint®; shelf: Primer Red Chalk Paint®.

Page 125 Washed-out Striped Drapes Wall: Emperor's Silk Chalk Paint® and Clear Soft Wax (see page 142); bookshelves: Paris Grey Chalk Paint®.

Page 127 Swedish Painted Blind Wall: Old White Wall Paint; stairs: Old White Chalk Paint®.

Page 131 Alphabet Transfer Banner Wall: Old White Wall Paint; skirting board: Old White Chalk Paint®; chair: English Yellow Chalk Paint® with Clear Soft Wax, upholstered in Emile & Graphite Coloured Linen.

Page 136 Random Stencil Wall Table: Antibes Green Chalk Paint® and Black Chalk Paint® Wax; chair: Antibes Green Chalk Paint®.

Page 142 Emperor's Silk Waxed Wall Chair: Provence Chalk Paint®; picture frame: Graphite Chalk Paint®.

Page 145 Washed Wood Floor: Amsterdam Green Chalk Paint®.

Page 147 Paris Grey Parquet Wall and skirting board: Aubusson Blue Wall Paint; chair: Château Grey and Greek Blue Chalk Paint®.

Page 151 Fabric Wall Wooden box: Aubusson Blue, Primer Red, and Burgundy Chalk Paint®.

Page 155 Rough and Luxurious Wall Chair: Paris Grey Chalk Paint® with Clear Soft Wax, upholstered in Aubusson & Provence, Emile & Graphite, and English Yellow & Antibes Green Coloured Linens, trim in Napoleonic Blue & Barcelona Orange Coloured Linen.

INDEX

ACKNOWLEDGMENTS

Many thanks to Ant and Tom at LASSCO architectural salvage (www.lassco.co.uk) for the radiogram, plaster cast, and plaque for the Textured Paint Radiogram (page 19), as well as the glass apothecary bottles for the Smooth and Textured Cabinet (page 27).

Many thanks to Nat and Ko at Gilt and Grain (www.giltandgrain.com) for the Western poster for the Frottage Wall (page 153) and help with other pieces.

Thanks also to Nkuku (www.nkuku.com/category/house-and-home/lighting) for providing the lamp base for the Crackled Lamp Base (page 57).

Thanks to Pentreath & Hall (www.pentreath-hall.com/accessories/alphabet-brush-pots.html) for the brush pots for the Making An Arc chest of drawers (page 39).

Many thanks to artist Andrew Walton (www.andrewwaltonartist.org.uk) for the loan of his painting displayed on the Emperor's Silk Waxed Wall (page 142) and Susan James for her upholstery (www.hessianandtwine.com) on various projects.

Many thanks to all my stockists all over the world for their continued support but, in particular, I'd like to thank Alfie Dehez of French Origin, in Cornwall, England, for her inspiration for the Stenciled and Hand-painted Chest of Drawers (pages 68–71).

When I said I was writing this book, everyone wondered how I could possibly do it, with my already tight schedule. I knew the answer: it is because I have an amazing team around me who, with their enthusiasm, warmth, sense of humor, and hard work, have made it possible.

Everyone at the warehouse where we have done much of the work is totally amazing in so many ways. Thank you! They helped me by finding furniture, lifting furniture, researching, painting, dyeing, washing, cutting, sawing, sewing, cleaning, finding flowers, making, mending, waxing, and making tea and coffee, as well as getting us lunch and a hundred other things.

Thank you to Christopher Drake, who has taken all the photographs in the book. Christopher has now worked on five books with me, and that's because he has almost endless patience, always makes the team laugh, is willing to get his hands dirty, and, of course, has a terrific eye and great ideas too!!

And, of course, there is THE BOOK TEAM!! Thank you very much Ann Tutt, Cal Dagul, Felix Sloan, Holly Jones, Rudi Howes, and Tim Fryer for being such stalwarts, through thick and thin, for being so skilful, capable, and helpful—and you kept smiling! I am very grateful!!

Also many thanks to Amy Honour, Charlotte Freeston, Sofka Smales, Hannah Simpson, Christopher Oswald, Joanna Lloyd, Thomas Instone, James Halfhide, and Dominic Hand for their help along the way. And lastly and, in particular, to Tanya Evans, my other half and personal assistant who did all the organizing!!

And, of course, as usual, thanks to my family—David, Henry, Hugo, Lizzy, Felix, Willow, and Rudy—for huge support and understanding throughout the whole process of getting a book done. I couldn't do it without you!